Praise for
How to Get Your Ideas Adopted (and Change the World)

"I love this book. I didn't realise it was going to be so interesting! It's very relevant to campaigning."
Andy Atkins, executive director, Friends of the Earth

"Wise and original."
Anthony Haynes, for the Association of MBAs

"I liked the down-to-earth, practical, hands-on approach to getting ideas accepted that this book offers."
Chris Moore, director, external affairs, Kodak

"The best book I've read in a long time!"
Richard Burkinshaw, European environmental strategy manager, Kellogg's

"Well written, interesting, imaginative and a mine of information."
Dr Meredith Belbin, founder of Belbin, the home of team roles

"This book will be invaluable for those who want to get their ideas – especially novel ones – accepted."
Professor Brian D. Josephson, Physics Nobel Laureate 1973

"According to Oscar Wilde, an idea that is not considered dangerous is unworthy of being called an idea at all. Anne Miller's book is full of ideas, dangerous ideas, and dangerous ideas about dangerous ideas. Enjoy. Embrace. Evangelize."
Professor Stephen Brown, Professor of Marketing Research, University of Ulster

"Never one to be daunted by the size of the challenge, Anne Miller inspires us all – whatever our business or purpose – to think beyond our normal limits and to create and innovate for competitive advantage and sustainable futures."
Professor Dame Sandra Dawson, Judge Business School, Cambridge

HOW TO GET
YOUR IDEAS
ADOPTED
(AND CHANGE
THE WORLD)

HOW TO GET
YOUR IDEAS
ADOPTED
(AND CHANGE
THE WORLD)

ANNE MILLER

Marshall Cavendish
Business

Copyright © 2009 Anne Miller

This paperback edition published in 2009 by:

Marshall Cavendish Limited
Fifth Floor
32–38 Saffron Hill
London EC1N 8FH
United Kingdom
T: +44 (0)20 7421 8120
F: +44 (0)20 7427 8121
E: sales@marshallcavendish.co.uk
www.marshallcavendish.co.uk

First hardback edition published in 2007 as *The Myth of the Mousetrap*

The right of Anne Miller to be identified as the author of this work has been
asserted by her in accordance with the Copyright, Designs and Patents Act 1988.

Copyright acknowledgements for photographs and other material appear
either beside the reproduced material, in the relevant endnotes, or in the
acknowledgements on page 203.

A CIP record for this book is available from the British Library

ISBN-13: 978-0-462-09929-3

Printed and bound in Great Britain by
CPI Bookmarque, Croydon CR0 4TD

For Tom

Contents

Preface to the new edition

WRITING A BOOK ABOUT HOW TO overcome the resistance to ideas was always going to be fraught with danger.

I felt that this was an important and much neglected topic, and one that would be of relevance to a wide range of people who were trying to get new ideas adopted. I saw that, in contrast to the myths that claim that the world will beat a path to your door for your good idea, the reality is that the newer and more important your idea, the more strongly it will be resisted and ignored. If I was right about this, my book risked sinking like a stone.

However, the key message of the book is that "Resistance is normal, so don't get demoralized, get smart." This meant that people would naturally be interested in how the book was received, which might be embarrassing.

The responses to the first edition were most encouraging. My first sign of the reactions to come was an email, a few days after the book launch, which started, "It's absolutely bloody brilliant!"

It rapidly became clear that I was right that this was a topic of great interest to a wide range of people. I got wildly enthusiastic feedback from entrepreneurs, environmentalists and engineers; chemists, clergy and campaigners; librarians, managers, novelists and parents. For all their differences, they were all people who were trying to get new ideas adopted.

In some cases they were trying to promote a new business, an idea or an invention, and were finding that the traditional marketing techniques didn't really seem adequate to unlock the deep-seated resistance that their ideas were facing.

Others were motivated by trying to make the world a slightly better place. Campaigners have well-proven tactics for influencing politicians and the public, but increasingly these were seeming inadequate in the face of complex global threats like climate change, food shortages and poverty.

The third group didn't necessarily see themselves as creative or as innovators, but were trying to deal with unwelcome changes that were being forced upon them. For example, the public library service is faced with a massive change in its role. In the past, information was scarce and hard to find, so librarians collected and classified it and made it available for the public. Today we have the opposite problem: information is readily available, but too much of it is biased, inaccurate, or blatantly fraudulent. Like it or not, library services around the world are having to develop a new vision of their role and change the way they do things in order to survive. For staff within the service, this means that many of them are faced with the unfamiliar problem of how to develop and spread new ideas and ways of working.

People in all three groups told me that it was exciting and inspiring to find a source of new insights into how to move their ideas forward. Interestingly, the more understanding people had of creativity and innovation, the more significant they tended to find the book.

The converse of this was that it was hard to get the mainstream press interested, because those with less experience of working with new ideas couldn't really see the point. As one BBC presenter pointed out to me, the concept that ideas are resisted doesn't really fit with the comfortable myth that you can have a "eureka moment" and immediately make your fortune. As discussed in Chapter 4, when ideas don't fit with the way someone sees the world, they usually get ignored.

The publisher and I persisted. I wrote articles, ran workshops, gave talks and answered emails, explaining the ideas to people and helping them relate them to the issues facing them. Often people found it quite shocking to realize why their ideas were being resisted, but became gleeful as they then realized there were proven techniques to help. This personal approach obviously has its limits: there is only a certain number of hours in the day. But it is proving very successful in developing a network of people who, in their own individual ways, are enthusing about the ideas to their colleagues and friends.

People are surprisingly skilful at misinterpreting new ideas to fit with their expectations, so we discovered that some people were misled by the original title *The Myth of the Mousetrap: How to get your ideas adopted (and change the world)*. On-line retailers helpfully categorized the book under "pest control". Others decided that it was just a book for (mad) inventors and hence not for them.

One of the key aspects of getting your ideas adopted is to hold fast to your inspiring vision, but be flexible and responsive: new ideas almost always need to be morphed to reach their true potential. This meant that, although we were fond of *The Myth...* as a title, we decided to pare it down for this new edition, changing it to simply *How to Get Your Ideas Adopted (and Change the World)*.

The ride so far has been occasionally frustrating, but overall fun and fulfilling. I look forward to the reception of the new edition with great interest.

Anne Miller
Autumn 2008

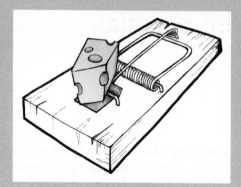

"Invent a better mousetrap and the world
will beat a path to your door"
(Anon.)

Introduction

"WHO'S SHE?" I HEARD THEM THINK, as a wave of locker doors shut along the corridor ahead of me, revealing a flutter of soft porn.

I was an 18-year-old student trainee at the turbo generator manufacturer C. A. Parsons, in the northeast of England, being led down the corridor into The Works to join 3,000 men. My career was beginning.

I had decided to study engineering two years earlier because I wanted to become a professional inventor. I was always passionate about being creative, but I knew I wasn't good enough at art to earn my living as an artist. Becoming an inventor sounded even better. It combined several things I was interested in: it would let me be creative, was grounded in science and might actually allow me make a difference in a way that my skills as an artist never would.

It was only much later that I realized I'd made this life-changing decision without really thinking about the implications of being a woman in a male-dominated profession. I suspect that one of these consequences, apart from having a lot of fun breaking people's stereotypes, was to make me sensitive to the ways in which we all balance asserting our individuality and conforming to the expectations of the group. This is important both in creativity, and in the way in which we get ideas adopted. Some have also suggested that I bring a particularly "female" perspective to the process of the adoption of ideas, focusing more on collaboration than competition, and on engaging support rather than overpowering opposition. This may be true, in the sense that I certainly seem to put more emphasis on these areas than many of my male colleagues. However, I am also very clear these are techniques that are equally valid in both male and female hands. The approach might even be more powerful when used by men, because it would be more unexpected, and, as we will see later, combining the unexpected with the familiar is an effective way to break through the earlier stages of blindness to new ideas.

The "lads" at C. A. Parsons gradually got used to me, and gave me an awesome introduction to the world of "heavy" engineering: a world in which even the nuts and bolts were so huge they had to be carried by crane. Although wild rumours circulated at intervals about what I was doing there it didn't put me off, and in due course I went to Cambridge University to read Engineering. After my degree I then spent the next 25 years as an engineer, innovator and technical consultant.

Having started my career at almost the largest possible scale, over the years I steadily moved towards designing smaller and smaller things, so one of my last developments was for a new way of helping people with diabetes measure their blood sugar, in which key components were so small we had to use a microscope to see them. I particularly liked designing products that people would handle and so developed a lot of power tools, as well as various hand-held medical, surgical and diagnostic devices.

Some developments were fun but ultimately rather unimportant, like the "gourmet" toaster or troubleshooting the manufacture of a new brand of "choc 'n' nut" coated choc ices one hot August. Others, like the computerized fire-fighting training school for the Royal Navy or the manufacturing machine for the Femidom (the surprisingly large female condom), help save lives. Some (39) of them were patented, and the patents were assigned to the companies that then owned and manufactured them. However, by far the largest proportion were never launched and never adopted, and have quietly faded away, except for a few souvenirs and photos.

In 1988, I was fortunate enough to be able to join with a group of colleagues and help set up a technology consultancy, run the way we thought it ought to be run. This became The Technology Partnership (later TTP Group),[1] led by a remarkable man, Dr Gerald Avison, who in his quiet but inimitable way set the tone for a company based on an inspiring mixture of partnership, ethics, autonomy and fun. This made for a very enjoyable, creative and successful business.

However, in 2000 I found that I was getting more and more interested in why some organizations and individuals were so much more effective in their creativity than others, and so I moved away from technology consultancy to set up a learning and development consultancy, The Creativity Partnership.[2] This grew into a fully independent business, focusing on helping organizations become more creative, building partnerships and running training courses and workshops. I found it very interesting combining my experience of innovation with ideas from the world of organizational development, because it gave me insights about why ideas are resisted, and what one can do about it.

In parallel with building up the Creativity Partnership, I became increasingly concerned about the way the threat of climate change was being ignored, so I was pleased when I had the opportunity to help set up the UK coalition of non-governmental organizations (NGOs), Stop Climate Chaos,[3] and get involved in its work to create a public mandate for political action on climate change.

The problem with ideas

This background has made me very aware of the power of creativity, and the value of good ideas. However, it has also made it very clear that the more radical and important the idea, the harder it is to get it adopted. The myth says, "Invent a better mousetrap and the world will beat a path to your door". But as every creative person knows, the reality is that they won't. They will deny that mice exist. They will deny that they need trapping. They will deny that your trap is any better than anyone else's. When finally you do win through, they will claim that they knew your idea was a winner all along. The same pattern repeats itself, whether the idea is a simple one like having some plants in the office, or a more complex one such as a new product concept, a new scientific theory or a campaign to change public attitudes.

You will only succeed in getting your idea truly adopted when you can break through these layers of blindness and denial to the point where people have genuinely taken ownership of the idea. This may need as much creativity, perceptiveness and skill as developing it in the first place, but all too often creative people pay only the most cursory attention to the process. When they fail, they either become discouraged and moan to their friends, or, alternatively, start waging war on their perceived opponents and trying to force their idea through. This is a shame, because neither is an effective tactic and failure means that the world loses the potential benefit of a good idea, while the originators lose out on the pleasure of seeing their ideas adopted.

It is important to point out that ideas do not need to be radical and earth-shattering to make a difference; even small incremental ideas will change the world immediately around you. For example, a junior manager at one of my client's businesses had the simple idea of putting a white board and some pens by the coffee machine. This transformed the way people discussed and shared ideas, as people from all levels in the company added suggestions and improvements to the current hot idea. When the board was full, she took a photo of it for the team to use, before wiping the board and putting up a new "trigger". This was just one step in a process of cultural transformation that lasted several years. Often, as the Japanese have shown in their products and manufacturing processes, the most successful way of making dramatic changes is to introduce a steady succession of incremental ideas in pursuit of the overall goal.

It always surprises me that there's no single word in the English language for such an important concept as "the process of getting ideas adopted". Some, like "selling" or "marketing", are too contractual and commercial, tending to imply that the idea is a completed package, maybe even covered by guarantee, just waiting to be married up with eager consumers. As we will see later, this is not true for ideas, because they almost always need to morph and evolve in the process of being adopted and made to work really well. I also find that some of the people who are most driven to use their creativity to make a difference are very uncomfortable with the concept of "marketing", because of their perception that it is about using spin and manipulation to sell trivia. Alternative words like "persuasion" and "influence" contain many useful elements of the concept, but are too vague to encapsulate a process that involves a mixture of inspiration and engagement around a specific idea.

The phrase "getting ideas adopted" is not succinct enough to be ideal, but I find the metaphor of an idea being like a child rather useful. Ideas, like children, start full of promise, but will need guidance, safety and space if they are to grow up healthily and fulfil their potential, even though this may well turn out to be quite different from what you first expected. Similarly, it needs careful thought, lots of work and emotional commitment if one is to be successful in getting either ideas or children successfully adopted.

It is important to pay attention to this because the world needs new ideas, both to resolve looming global threats like climate change or global terrorism, but also on a smaller and more local scale in families, communities and business.

Unfortunately, in many cases it is becoming harder and harder to use your creativity to make a difference. As organizations merge and grow in response to the economic pressures of globalization, many develop increasingly target-driven, risk-averse and controlling cultures. This is making them more and more dysfunctional in how they deal with creativity, so even though they are desperate for new ideas, it is increasingly difficult for the creative people within them to get their ideas to see the light of day. If you are a junior employee in this position it may be difficult to do much about the negativity and bureaucratization around you. However, you can take things into your own hands: rather than feeling frustrated and stuck, focus some of your creativity, skill and energy on being clever about how you get your ideas adopted. The result will be more satisfying for you, and better for your colleagues and the company.

Using this book

Getting ideas adopted is a fascinating and complex art. This book does not attempt to be an encyclopaedia, or to cover all possible issues and techniques; rather, it sets out to explore how you can give your ideas a better chance, deflate resistance and engage supporters.

This book is primarily for creative practitioners, so it assumes that you know how to encourage the flow of ideas: the problem is just how to turn seed ideas into great ideas and get them adopted. Sometimes these will be your own ideas, but in other situations you may just want to get a group of people to recognize that they have a problem so they start looking for ways to resolve it. As we will see later, rather than trying to force-feed people with your own idea for a solution, very often this more sophisticated approach is a better way of triggering the change you want.

I find creativity fascinating, because although ideas may start with the creative insight of one individual, they won't be adopted unless, by the end of the process, they relate to the needs and norms of the wider social group. This means that, as in so many things, you have to consider both the "internal" factors, such as whether you and your idea are worth paying attention to, as well as the "external" aspects, like why people are resisting it.

Recognizing this, the book is divided into two parts, exploring in turn the "internal" and the "external" aspects of the process.

Part 1 focuses on the "internal" aspects of the process, covering the key issues you will need to think about to get your idea into shape and give it the best possible chance of getting adopted. There are three key elements of this: firstly, understanding the normality of resistance. Secondly, understanding the way in which the very personality characteristics that help our creativity often make people reluctant to adopt our ideas. Some may find this difficult territory, but for those with the honesty to accept that some of the problems they face may be of their own making, I am including an extract from the well-validated Myers-Briggs psychometric test to help you explore and address your own personal strengths and weaknesses. The third element focuses on the practical details of developing ideas that people might actually want. Much of this is based on my experience running innovation teams and developing technological innovations.

Part 2 focuses on the more "external" aspects of the process, looking in turn at how to overcome the four stages of resistance, when people are in turn "blind", "frozen", "interested" and "integrated". These are very different stages. Initially, when people are "blind" they seem to be wilfully ignoring our idea: we try to tell them about it, but see their eyes glaze over. In the second stage they may be aware of the idea, but they make all sorts of excuses to avoid admitting that it's important or needs action. It's only when they reach the third stage, after we have succeeded in unfreezing them, that they become actively interested in knowing about our idea (whether or not they will like it when they hear about it). In the fourth and final stage our task becomes one of helping our recipient integrate the idea into their lives, otherwise we'll find a few weeks later that they have slipped back into their old patterns of behaviour and forgotten all about it.

An idea is only truly adopted when it feels comfortable and natural and has become part of the way someone sees the world.

This model of the resistance to ideas is based on concepts that are relatively well known in the field of organizational development. However, in the field of creativity and innovation this model is virtually unknown, even though it makes immediate intuitive sense to most creative people.

One of the main reasons I wanted to write this book is because I've seen so many creative people get unnecessarily frustrated because they can't get their ideas to see the light of day. This is never easy, but I hope this book will help.

Note that this book assumes that, like most creative people, once you have understood the basic principles, you would prefer to use them to create your own solution, rather than follow a defined step-by-step process for "guaranteed" success, so beloved of "how-to" books. It therefore contains lots of examples and stories and experiments to illustrate techniques that I have found important and useful from a wide range of disciplines. These include advertising, anthropology, campaigning, cognitive psychology, creativity studies, economics, linguistics, marketing communications, management theory, neuroscience, organizational development, personality profiling, philosophy, politics, presentation skills, psychotherapy, social psychology, story telling, technological innovation and "Web 2.0".

This book includes a lot of ideas, so it is easy to be enjoyably overwhelmed and fail to remember any of them. It therefore concludes with a space for you to note down the three key ideas that you want to remember from each chapter in the book. The table also includes my own favourites, but your choice will depend on your ideas, environment, personality and experience.

Anne Miller

PART

1

Getting into shape

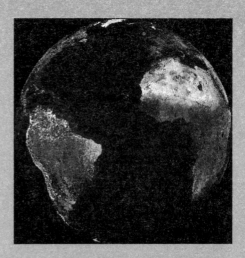

The challenge of ideas

WE ALL TEND TO ASSUME that it will be as obvious to others as it is to us that we have a great idea. Unfortunately, if you wait for the world to beat a path to your door, you're likely to have a long and lonely wait, because the more important and creative your idea, the more strongly it is likely to be resisted.

Although experiencing resistance isn't a guarantee that you have a brilliant idea, as this chapter discusses, you shouldn't get dispirited if it happens.

Resistance is normal

The first thing to remember is that resistance is normal, although you would never know it if you just looked at the success stories. Once an idea has been accepted, or an invention proven a success, it's amazing just how quickly everyone starts saying that they knew that it was a good idea all along.

The 350-year-old idea

When you look at a map of the Atlantic, it seems blindingly obvious today that the shapes of Africa and South America fit together, as if they were once joined. But the idea was only accepted in 1965, nearly 350 years after it was first suggested.

As far back as 1620, when Sir Francis Bacon studied the maps of the world drawn by Flemish geographers, such as Ortelius, he noticed the similarity in the coastlines of Africa and South America. He commented that this "cannot be by chance".[4]

At the time, the common belief was that the earth was fundamentally unchanged since its creation in 4004 BC.[5] The power of the Catholic Church made it dangerous to challenge this, so inconvenient facts like marine fossils on mountain tops tended to be accredited to the Deluge. During the Enlightenment of the eighteenth century it became accepted that the earth was created very much earlier, and that it had changed substantially since its creation. However, well into the twentieth century there was still a tacit assumption that something as massive as a continent would remain in a fixed position. It was hard to explain why very similar species were found on both sides of the Atlantic, but the prevailing theory was that there had once been a land bridge connecting Brazil and Africa, which had been flooded when the earth cooled and the land sank.

It was only in the early twentieth century that the theory of continental drift was suggested by Alfred Wegener, an explorer and respected lecturer in meteorology and astronomy at the University of Marburg in Germany. One day in the autumn of 1911, he had been browsing in the university library and had come across a paper that listed the fossils of identical plants and animals that had been discovered on both sides of the Atlantic. He became curious and started looking for more examples of similarities, which he soon found. For instance, not only do the coastlines of South America and Africa look as if they fit together, but the geological features often match too. The Appalachian mountains of eastern North America match with the Scottish Highlands, while the geology of the Karroo area of South Africa fits with that of the Santa Catarina area of Brazil. In other cases, the fossils showed that when the plants were growing the local climate must have been radically different from today, as there are fossil ferns on the island of Spitzbergen in the Arctic and coal deposits in the Antarctic.

Wegener was very bright, insightful and independent, but it was probably his background in the newly emerging science of meteorology that helped him come up with the remarkable insight that it wasn't just weather that could change on a global scale – maybe the continents themselves were moving? On an expedition to Greenland in 1906 he had noticed that the longitudinal calculations his party had made differed from earlier ones that had been calculated from measurements made in 1823 and 1870, and he later used these figures to estimate the rate at which the continents were moving. Even though these estimates were wildly excessive because of inaccuracies in the measurements, they helped reinforce his belief in the correctness of his idea.

On 6 January 1912, Wegener delivered an address to the Geological Association in Frankfurt proposing his theory: the continents had once been together, but had since drifted to their current positions.

It was considered ludicrous.

He continued developing the theory; gathering evidence and allies in the face of hostility and derision until his premature death in 1930 on an expedition to Greenland, aged fifty. In his obituaries he was acclaimed as a meteorologist, explorer, teacher and a brilliant academic, but his idea of continental drift was dismissed as a bizarre fantasy and an aberration in an otherwise exemplary life.

Although today it seems barely conceivable that it was so recently considered a heresy, it was only in 1965 that most of the scientific community finally became convinced that Wegener's theory was broadly correct, even though in retrospect one would have thought it had been visually obvious for the past 350 years.

The rejection rate

Wegener's frustrating experience is far from unusual, except perhaps in the sheer length of time it took for the fundamental idea that the continents fit together to become generally accepted.

Telephones, talking movies and the Beatles were all initially rejected:

"This telephone has far too many shortcomings to be seriously considered as a means of communication. The device is inherently of no value to us."
Western Union internal memo, 1876

"Who the hell wants to hear actors talk."
H. M. Warner (founder of Warner Brothers) rejecting the concept of movies with sound, 1927

"We don't like their sound, and guitar music is on the way out."
Decca Recording Co. rejecting the Beatles, 1962

It's easy to think that people are stupid if they turn down our ideas, but as these rejections show, in many cases the individuals doing the rejection are far from stupid and are multi-millionaires to prove it. Rejection is a fact of life for all creative people.

One of my first jobs as a young engineer was to develop a "gourmet toaster". This made excellent toast, crispy on the outside and soft and luscious on the inside, just like the toast I made as a child using a toasting fork in front of the fire.

The lads in the workshop thought it was a great product, and were thrilled to "help" with my testing programme by eating six loaves of hot buttered toast a day. However, the toaster never got launched. Even though it made incomparable toast, it was a bit expensive for our client's rather downmarket brand, and the elements in it were so powerful that there was a slight risk that people might get cataracts from using it. We could probably have solved this problem by changing the design a little, but in retrospect I can understand why we failed to win the argument. You don't really want to go blind from eating toast.

I wasn't alone in wasting my efforts. At least 90% of commercial product-development projects never see the light of day, even if they're well run and well resourced.

Even for something as simple as a new sandwich variety, only 60–70% of ideas proposed by the supermarket to the manufacturer are launched, and only 20% are still on sale a year later.[6]

The chances of success are much lower if the idea is genuinely new, rather than just a new variant of an existing product. For example, one study of the "universal" success rate of ideas for substantially "new to the world" products in corporations, in a variety of industries, showed that of three thousand raw, unwritten ideas, only three hundred were actually submitted in written form. Development work started on small-scale feasibility projects for only 125 of these, resulting in only 1.7 launches, and only one of those was a success.[7] Overall the success rate from idea to commercial success was just 0.03%.

Our ideas may fail for all sorts of reasons: they may not work, we may be wrong in assuming that we've created something that will be useful to people, or we may just run out of money or energy before we've succeeded in getting it to the stage when others can see the idea's promise. However, even if we have a good idea and all the resources we need, we may still fail to get it adopted.

Unfortunately, some of the factors that help us have creative ideas also make it harder for us to get those ideas adopted.

The creative outsider

One of the difficulties of creativity is that often it's our unusual experience that enables us to come up with an important new idea. However, the danger is that the group we are trying to influence will very often see us as a threatening outsider, and will club together to resist us, unless we're very skilful.

Wegener had this problem because the geological community was very tightly knit and specialist, and he wasn't even a geologist, but a meteorologist. Secondly, he was German, and in the aftermath of the First World War all Germans were viewed with suspicion. Worse still, he was a cross-disciplinary in a time when many scientific schools were jealous of their territories. He insisted on challenging botanists, biologists and geologists to abandon cherished beliefs and to think across the territorial lines they had worked hard to develop and protect. Although today this sort of cross-disciplinary approach is seen as fundamental for many fields, at the time the boundaries between scientific branches were newly created, and so this caused particular offence. As one of Wegener's supporters later explained, "To work on subjects which fall outside the traditionally defined bounds of a science naturally exposes one to being regarded with mistrust."

Even though he was brilliant, Wegener repeatedly failed to get a professorship in his home country, only succeeding when he moved to Graz in Austria. The reason given for his failure to gain an academic Chair was always the same; he was "interested in matters that lay outside [the Chair's] terms of reference".

It wasn't long before the established authorities closed ranks against him.[8] He never understood the depth of resistance to his thinking. Continental drift was received not merely as a mistaken idea but as an evil that jeopardized the credibility of geology as a science and the professional reputation of anyone who espoused it.

This experience of being an outsider is a common problem for creative people, because as we will see later, it's easier to produce creative ideas if you are an "interested outsider", as "insiders" tend to see everything through the lens of their expectations, which makes it difficult for them to come up with new ideas. However, the downside of being an outsider is that you will have to be particularly skilful in how you go about getting your new ideas accepted. As we'll see in Part 2, if you are using unfamiliar language and basing your ideas on unfamiliar ways of thinking about the world, people will often seem bizarrely blind to your idea until you can worm your way through their protective shields.

One might think that it was the scientific evidence that finally convinced people about his ideas, but it is noticeable that Wegener's early allies were people who had travelled and seen their homeland's familiar rock strata and fossils thousands of miles from home – this was so surprising that they demanded explanations. As we'll see later, this sort of emotionally intense first-hand experience is often more important than any scientific case in convincing sceptics of the need for a new idea.

Wegener's detractors often claimed that they couldn't accept his ideas because he couldn't explain what made the plates move. However, this probably wasn't the major problem, because ironically, as the US Geological Survey points out,[9] even in 2007 one of the chief outstanding questions is still the one Wegener failed to resolve: "What is the nature of the forces propelling the plates?"

Equally, the fossil evidence was no stronger in 1965 than it had been in 1930. It did, however, become easier for Wegener's ideas to gain acceptance after his death because of the discovery of the Mid-Atlantic Ridge, growing evidence for the spread of the Atlantic and the development of the new theory of plate tectonics.[10]

Wegener's supporters, such as South African Alexander Du Toit, were gathering evidence that could have been very influential, but the way in which they tried to advance his cause often only made things worse, emphasizing Wegener's position as an outsider.

In 1944, Chester Longwell – a prominent and distinguished geologist, as well as Chair of the department of Geology at Yale – was interested in Wegener's hypothesis, although he was still open minded about whether it was right. He discussed the controversy in the *American Journal of Science*, looking at some of the possible reasons why supporters like Alexander Du Toit were facing resistance.[11] He commented that part of the problem was that they tended to make wild generalizations that swept aside inconvenient facts and, in their enthusiasm, made many mistakes that were obvious to people with more specialist knowledge. As one prominent geologist said of Wegener's book, "It is at least fifty per cent dross, but it contains also some pure gold for anyone who looks for it honestly."

The "dross" and obvious mistakes meant that people tended to condemn the whole hypothesis out of hand, so Longwell urged Wegener's supporters to remember that they had "a human audience, endowed with limited time, patience, and objectivity". This is good advice to many of us today. It's very easy to get so excited about our idea that we "spam" our audience with much too much information on it, too soon: quite possibly when they are in the middle of doing something else, or just want to go home. As we will see later, it's much more effective to start by teasing out their interest.

With us or against us

It also did not help that Du Toit seemed to sense a strongly entrenched opposition in what he called "current geology". There were certainly some on both sides of the argument who were rigidly entrenched in their views, but by 1944 there was a growing number of scientists who were willing to consider the theory. Unfortunately, the combative atmosphere made it less likely that the ideas would readily be adopted, even by the open minded. As Longwell pointed out in the closing months of the Second World War: "Zealous believers commonly follow the motto, 'He that is not for us is against us'... It does not help the cause to accuse all its critics of 'orthodoxy', with the implication that this state of mind is as unworthy as fascism."

The phrase "with us or against us" has an uncanny and worrying echo today. For example, when George Bush told Congress on 4 October 2001 that America was building a coalition to "defeat evil", he said, "Either you're with us, or against us."[12] He was applauded by his audience, many of whom probably realized that he was paraphrasing Christ.[13] However, in the wider world outside Congress and outside America, the absolutist nature of the phrase triggered alarm. Where was the scope for neutrality? Where was the scope for people to admire some aspects of America and its policies, but dislike others?

It is noteworthy that although George Bush told President Chirac of France a month later that he was going to be using the phrase in his forthcoming address to the UN, the final speech wisely made no reference to it.[14]

Just as in Wegener's day, being combative may make your supporters feel good, but it does nothing to encourage people who are teetering on the edge of being interested in your ideas.

The nature of ideas

Even without the problems of being seen as an outsider, there's something about the nature of ideas that makes them hard to get across.

As discussed below, this is firstly because ideas are hard to communicate. Secondly, it's because ideas drive our behaviour in deep and fundamental ways, so we're understandably protective of what ideas we will adopt. Thirdly, ideas involve us emotionally, so there are surprisingly close parallels between an idea and a belief.

The imperfect copy

The first problem about creative ideas is that they are hard to communicate, but often we fail to realize this. Our idea seems so wonderful and complete in our own minds that we believe all we need to do is explain it to someone, and they will be sold on it too. However, this doesn't work.

This is because ideas start by being intangible, intuitive and often a bit ambiguous. As Sir Nevill Mott, winner of the 1977 Nobel Prize in Physics, once said, "You suddenly see: it must be like this. That's intuition … but you can't convince anybody else. This certainly happened to me in the work for which I got my Nobel Prize. It took me years to get my stuff across."

Ideas exist in the mind, and quite possibly, initially, only in our minds. This means that someone has to be able to visualize your idea to assess it, and even then, the idea that they envisage may not necessarily be the one that you were trying to convey to them.

Most people who have ever been involved in the product development process in big companies will be familiar with the saga of the tree swing.

What the customer wanted

What marketing suggested

What engineering designed

What maintenance installed

It's not just in industry that we find this difficulty in envisaging someone else's idea.

Because ideas start by being abstract, they are inevitably much more difficult to explain to someone than when we have a tangible completed product, so we often try to make our ideas more concrete by gathering supporting data and hardware. Wegener and Du Toit assembled data on the distribution of fossil reptiles in South Africa and South America. Alexander Graham Bell built a prototype telephone. The Beatles did a test record with Decca in London.

This makes the idea more tangible and easier to communicate, so it helps people feel that they understand it. However, almost inevitably, the prototypes, data and examples we show won't incorporate the full splendour of our vision for the idea, so the idea may then be rejected because of its obvious shortcomings, just as Western Union did to Alexander Graham Bell's telephone.

The first commercial telephone, 1877
Courtesy of AT&T Archives and History Center

When you look at the first commercial telephone, the misgivings were understandable, as it was almost impossible to use. It was nothing more than a wood box about the size of a shoe box, with one hole on the end for both talking and listening. This resulted in dizzying head turning when having a conversation. Some of the first instructions stated, "When you aren't talking, you should be listening!"

Plato thought the gap between the vision for an idea and tangible reality was so fundamental to the nature of an idea that he defined an idea as being "an eternally existing pattern, of which individual things in any class are but imperfect copies".[15]

Although this is a very specific definition of the concept of an "idea", experienced creative people everywhere know the feeling that even the final embodiment of their idea will be "but an imperfect copy" of their original vision. Many creative people are so sensitive to the risk of having an "imperfect copy" of their idea rejected that they refine it endlessly and never actually have the courage to show it to anyone. Alternatively, the fear of producing an "imperfect copy" can result in us holding far too closely to our original vision, refusing to modify it whether we are right or wrong.

This means that part of the art of getting your ideas implemented is in judging when to hold firm to your original vision, and when to compromise.

Ideas drive our attitudes and behaviour

The second reason why people are cautious about adopting ideas is because ideas can be dangerous, influencing our behaviour in ways we may or may not want.

A First World War hero like my grandfather was willing to sacrifice his life for his country because he believed that this was the right thing to do: he was doing his duty.[16] Similarly, a 21st-century suicide bomber might be convinced that he was doing the right thing in walking onto a bus full of schoolchildren with a bomb, even though some years earlier he would have reacted to the idea with the same horror as the rest of the population.

These are both very dramatic examples of the consequences of adopting an idea, and in most situations the consequences are much less serious. Nevertheless, they can still create fundamental changes in the way we think and behave.

Sometimes this is the result of a deliberate campaign. In the early 1920s, the Lambert pharmaceutical company wanted to increase the market for their antibacterial liquid, which had been used as a general antiseptic since the 1880s. They brought in advertising man Gordon Seagrove to discuss how it could be done. He and his colleagues were listening to a presentation from the company's chemist describing its uses, when the chemist used a word that no one knew: "halitosis". Wisely, rather than pretending they understood his jargon, they asked what he meant. When he explained that it meant unpleasant breath, they immediately realized that this was a hook they could hang their campaign on.

Seagrove and his collaborator Milton Feasley developed this idea and launched a campaign that played heavily on the fear of people's reactions to a halitosis sufferer. One of their most famous ads featured Edna, approaching 30, who was "often a bridesmaid, never a bride" because she suffered from halitosis, a disorder so personal that "even your closest friends won't tell you".

The campaign was very successful, increasing sales of Listerine from $100,000 p.a. to $4 million in just six years.

Although bad breath had been a fact of life for thousands of years, Seagrove and Feasley created the idea of the social stigma – without the stigma, very few were interested in buying the mouthwash.

Similarly, people have driven and crashed cars while drunk since cars were first invented, but it took a deliberate campaign to introduce the idea that this was socially unacceptable. In the UK this started in 1979, when the government first published statistics of drink-related fatalities, kicking off a series of "don't drink and drive" campaigns which were very successful in introducing the idea that it was socially unacceptable to drink and drive. Whereas in the 1970s a polite middle-class host would be offering guests "one for the road", by the 1990s they wouldn't think of having a party without soft drinks available for the drivers. Although this didn't eliminate the problem, it had a dramatic impact, so that by 2003 only one-third as many people were being killed in drink-related car crashes as in 1979.

Sometimes new ideas develop and spread in society, despite the efforts of formal campaigns. For example, the ease of electronic copying seems to be driving a change in ideas about the nature of theft.

In one seminar I run on creating and exploiting intellectual property, I start the discussion of copyright by asking the students how many of them have stolen someone's wallet.[17] There's usually embarrassed laughter, but only one person has ever put their hand up. I then ask how many people have software or files on their computer where, "just possibly", they may not have permission from the copyright owner. There's another laugh, but a forest of hands raise: virtually the whole class will admit it. In an age in which electronic copying is effectively free, our ideas about the morality of breaching copyright have changed from the days when books had to be laboriously typeset by hand. As a result of adopting this relatively new idea, people will now freely commit a crime, and admit to it in public.

The music and film industry is trying to fight back against illegal downloads and piracy with an advertising campaign and prosecutions, but so far it has had little success in changing attitudes because people don't believe it's morally wrong. Initially the FACT (Federation Against Copyright Theft) campaign tried a quite muscular approach, focusing on the fact that piracy is illegal. This was successful to the extent that people became aware it was criminal, but as even the industry insiders admitted, it didn't do a lot to change attitudes – people don't like feeling bullied.

As a result, in May 2007 they started a new approach, focusing more on the immorality of ripping off artists and local businesses. This more subtle approach is likely to be much more effective, because people want to feel that they make their own decisions.

Because ideas are such an important part of who we are and how we behave, we can be very protective about whether or not we adopt one: trying to impose your ideas on others doesn't work.

Emotional commitment

The third difficult characteristic is that we become emotionally involved in our ideas. In some organizations this would be treated with horror, but the reality is that, although we can't forget our rationality if we want to develop ideas that will actually work, emotional involvement is positively helpful to our drive and creativity. Many far-sighted, innovative companies recognize this, and try to encourage it.

For example, 3M is a company with an enviable reputation for innovation. A few years ago, Professor Edward Roberts from the MIT Sloan School of Management presented his impressions of 3M senior management's views on the preconditions for successful "internal venturing". This is a process in which new business ventures are developed within a bigger company, trying to simultaneously get the benefits of being both a small (buzzy) and large (rich) corporation. One of the five key things they looked for in their creative people was "emotional involvement and commitment".[18]

This emotional commitment is important, but it also has less helpful consequences. For example, I once had a very able young (male) engineer in tears because our client had decided not to put his invention into production; it seemed to him to be such a perfect fit to their needs and he had invested so much of himself in developing it that the rejection was almost unbearable. It takes a lot to make a man cry, but this feeling of desolation is very common. As a manager, I found that when this happened, the most helpful thing to do was to talk through the reasons for the rejection and then find the "rejectee" a new and interesting creative challenge to take their mind off the pain.

For some creative people it becomes an article of faith that their idea will work. If you have no clear proof that your idea will succeed, faith can be useful, because sometimes it is all you have to sustain you in your pursuit of a visionary dream. However, it becomes less helpful if your faith in the idea means that it starts to take on the trappings of a religious cult.

Creative people can be as absorbed in and emotionally committed to their ideas as the religious believer is to their faith. The parallel is closer than we might think because generally speaking philosophers see a proposition or a hunch in which we have some emotional or psychological investment as a "belief".[19] This would be distinct from a mere hypothesis which we may not care about one way or the other. "Imagine there's an elephant in the next room" could be a hypothesis, in which we have no particular investment. "I believe there's an elephant in the next room" does have that investment.

Once we start to think of important creative ideas as involving the same level of emotional commitment as religious belief, it becomes clear why an idea's originator may find it hard to understand why other people can't see how wonderful it is, why doubters start to be seen as heretics, and why people may be cautious about adopting new ideas.

We might well be willing to test drive a new car for a week, but if you want to persuade a left-wing activist to try subscribing to a right-wing newspaper, a fashion conscious teenager that it's OK to go out without her makeup on, or a cautious manufacturing manager to try out your bright idea in his factory, telling them to "just try it" is as fruitless as asking someone to try believing in a new religion for a week.

You will have to be much more sophisticated in how you go about getting them to dip their toes in the water and consider your ideas.

The death and rebirth of marketing?

As we've seen, it's part of the nature of new ideas that they get resisted, and the more important they are, the more strongly they are likely to be resisted. Recognizing this is an important first step, because it helps you keep your morale up and persist through the frustrating and exhausting process of getting ideas adopted.

However, I find that many creative people believe two very unhelpful myths about how to get their ideas adopted. The first is, "Isn't it just marketing?" I believe that, while not exactly incorrect, this point of view encourages an ineffective approach.

The second unhelpful myth is that marketing is something vaguely distasteful and lacking in integrity, so people are reluctant to get involved. As one campaigner put it, when thinking about how to spread her ideas, "Oh dear, does that mean we'll have to get into marketing?"

This negative attitude is quite widespread, and is particularly strong amongst creative individuals in groups as disparate as engineers and campaigners. For both, there's a sense that the inherent truth and beauty of their idea should win through, without sinking to the level of the spin and manipulation they see being used to sell trivia all around them. Most professionals in the so-called "creative industries" of marketing, media and advertising will have come across this and some may feel it themselves (as we will see later with some of the pioneers in the Marketing 2.0? section on page 25).

For creative people in general, this combination of attitudes is bad news, because it means that all they do about getting their ideas adopted is either try a few half-hearted attempts and then give up and moan when they get ignored, or else shout ever louder and get increasingly frustrated in waging war on their opponents.

Neither works.

The death of marketing

The disquiet about some aspects of marketing is not confined to maverick inventors and campaigners. Even though US ad revenues were an amazing

$264 billion in 2004 (2.2% of US GDP),[20] so one would have thought the ad people knew what they were doing, there is a surprising degree of disquiet in the industry: it has some fundamental problems.

Mark Earls is a leading figure in the London advertising scene, with impeccable credentials. He is the former Executive Group Planning Director at Ogilvy London, one of the UK's leading communications groups, and has spent his whole career in the advertising and marketing industry. In 2002 he announced "the death of marketing".[21] This was recognized in the industry as being broadly correct, although there was more debate about his proposed solution.

His analysis of the problem can be summed up as follows:

Firstly, there's too much of everything and we (in the affluent part of the world) already have most of the things we really need. As many of the differences between products are trivial, the choice we get is bewildering, rather than empowering. Does it really help our lives to have a choice of 50 toothbrushes at our local supermarket?

Secondly, consumers are becoming savvy activists, rather than passive, grateful "consumers". We are bombarded with typically 3,000 commercial messages per day, but we have become so skilled in filtering them out that we remember hardly any of them.

The traditional "interruption" approach to marketing means that to get people's attention advertising campaigns have to shout ever louder. They do this either by buying saturation coverage, or by being ever more outrageous, so sadomasochism is used to sell pot noodles, the faces of death row prisoners to sell clothes. A new household cleaner was promoted recently with a flood of TV advertising and a "presenter" who literally shouted at the viewers. As the campaigns get ever more odious, more people switch off.

On 23 May 2005, Stuart Elliot discussed the advertising industry's problem in the *New York Times* and pointed out that technology has helped shift power to the consumer, and we are using it to avoid ads. "The origins of the industry's current problems are many: the dot-com bust, the fallout from 9/11 and the explosive growth of technologies that help consumers avoid ads – like digital video recorders, iPods and satellite radio."

What's worse (for the industry), we are starting to lose the trust we once had in our corporations. Naomi Klein's book *No Logo* was a powerful statement of the idea that consumers should stand up against the big brand-name corporations. This was echoed by anti-globalization protestors around the world, while scandals such as Enron in the USA or pension mis-selling in the UK only reinforce the view that corporations can't be trusted.

More fundamentally, insiders are starting to argue that advertising doesn't work. Al Ries, best-selling co-author of *The Fall of Advertising and the Rise of PR*, says, "In eight years, General Motors spent $23 billion on advertising. What did they get for their money? They lost six per cent of market share, that's what they got – from thirty-four per cent in 1995 to twenty-eight per cent in 2001."[22]

He points out that many of the most successful brands use very little advertising. For example, Starbucks spent less than $10 million in advertising in its first ten years. That's less than $1 million a year, a trivial amount for a national brand. He quotes Howard Schultz, CEO of Starbucks, as saying, "It is difficult to launch a product through consumer advertising because customers don't really pay attention as they did in the past. I look at the money spent on advertising and it surprises me that people still believe they are getting returns on their investments."

This is not to say that no advert can ever work: clearly some do, but people are beginning to question why the publicity campaigns that work do so. There's a growing feeling that it's to do with involving people, rather than just communicating *at* them, and with the integrity and truth behind the message. If a company doesn't live up to its brand values it's playing with fire, in the same way that Nike lost 50% of its brand value in 1993. This started when New York kids decided that they didn't like the way their trainers were being made in sweatshops in Southeast Asia, and the protest then spread to consumers round the world.

Marketing 2.0?

This sort of thinking is pioneering a new approach to marketing and communications, which is all about involvement rather than interruption. This has been strongly influenced by the interactivity of the World Wide Web. Whereas initially the Internet was seen as an electronic version of a cross between a postal service and a publisher, as we'll see in Chapter 8, the most successful websites today are interactive, getting millions of users to develop and share content, whether it's Wikipedia or MySpace. Just as this new way of using the Internet is referred to as Web 2.0, one pioneer of the new way of thinking about marketing told me, early in 2007, "It's too early for the movement to have a name yet, but I bet it will end up being called Marketing 2.0."[23]

Focusing on "involvement rather than interruption" is valuable when trying to create a market for a "me-too" new product, but because of the involving nature of ideas, it's even more important when trying to get a radically new idea adopted.

This applies whether your idea is world changing, or just something small. For example, if you want to get your partner to go with your idea of trying a new holiday destination, most people recognize that your chances of success are much higher if you are flexible and prepared to compromise, rather than being fixated on every detail of what you want to do, and where you want to go.

This new approach draws on ideas from traditional sales and marketing, but goes deeper into the area of our beliefs and our blind-spots, into what motivates us to get involved and apply our creativity, and how we integrate ideas into our lives. As the most successful marketers already know, this is both harder and easier than the traditional approach. Harder because it is trying, in some small way, to change the way people see the world, to get them to want to use soap rather than just switch brands of soap. It can also be easier, because if you are genuinely involving people, they will respond with their creativity and involvement too.

Finally, if your idea is genuinely trying to make the world a better place, you will also have the advantage that this will tend to shine through and will attract supporters, in a way that the commercial sales gimmick never can.

Much better inventing at home
(The Professor's invention for peeling potatoes)

CHAPTER

2

Understanding our creativity

CREATIVITY IS A MYSTERIOUS AND WONDERFUL THING, but before we start looking at how to deal with resistance to our ideas from others, we need to start by making sure our own house is in order. We need to recognize and value our creativity, using the gifts we have as skilfully as we can.

I firmly believe that we are all creative, although like any human ability it's expressed in different ways and at different levels by different people. It's also influenced by the environment we're in, the opportunities we have and the support we get. Unfortunately, this means that some people acquire the unjustified belief that they are uncreative, when in reality it is probably just that they haven't yet had the opportunities to realize how creative they are.

Others of us are lucky enough to have found an environment in which our creativity can flourish. We find it absorbing, fun and rewarding. Nevertheless, it's very frustrating when your bright ideas never seem to see the light of day. Sometimes this is because of the natural resistance from others, whether rational or irrational, but the brutal reality is that some of the problems we face will be our own fault. Creative people have a reputation for being "quite impossible", and sadly there's some truth in this. All too often we behave in ways that make it less likely that we will succeed in getting our ideas adopted.

This chapter starts by exploring how we can recognize our true creativity and nurture it. It then explores some of the less helpful side effects of a creative personality and what we can do to improve our chances.

Creative self-confidence

Often when I'm working with groups I will meet someone who will initially deny that they are creative, but then, after a bit of coaching and encouragement, will produce some super ideas. Their self image was clearly wrong and this was handicapping them.

This lack of "creative self-confidence" is very common, and it matters.

It's creative self-confidence that gives us the courage to speak out about an idea. Without it, we assume that our idea will be useless, won't work or that someone else will have thought of it first. With it, we believe that there's a possibility that our idea will be new and useful, and so we tell someone about it. Our idea now has a chance, and one that it wouldn't have had if we had remained silent.

There are various reasons people falsely lack creative self-confidence. It can be the experience of previous rejections, bad experiences in school or what I call the "the myth of the Eureka Moment".

The first reason can be dismissed very quickly because, as will become very clear in this book, rejection is a fact of life for all creative people. In fact, the more creative your idea, the more vigorously it's likely to get resisted.

Bad school experiences

School experiences are a major source of a lack of creative self-confidence. All too often I meet people who deny that they are creative. When I ask how they know this, they say something like "The art teacher told me so when I was twelve."

That's not an adequate reason to handicap oneself for life. It could have had more to do with an overworked teacher being unimpressed by a less-than-wholehearted effort, rather than any true reflection of a lack of creative artistic ability. Even if true, the comment would only apply to your artistic creativity in the school environment.

This is because creativity is "domain specific". Someone who is highly creative in one particular domain of knowledge can very often be cautious and conventional in other areas. A tax accountant and an artist may both be highly creative in their own fields, but useless in the other's. Sometimes even subtle differences between domains can be very important. For example, it's quite common for people who feel comfortable and creative addressing an audience of 300 to freeze in front of a group of six, or vice versa.

To be creative in a domain of knowledge, we have to be interested in it. This is unlikely to happen unless there is a reasonable fit with our skills and we are exposed to the field in a way that gives us the opportunity to be creative.

Some schools and teachers are utterly inspiring, bringing out the creativity and imagination of the students, whatever their discipline. Worryingly, however, many teachers and exam boards seem to confine creativity to rigidly defined areas like the art class or creative writing exercises. Whereas in research and development departments in industry, engineers do experiments to satisfy their curiosity and find out something new – like "how well does the prototype of my bright idea work?" – in school science, students often labour through experiments to replicate the theorem that the teacher has written on the board. It's not surprising they find this boring.

I was once talking to a senior manager at a UK examinations board about the opportunity for them to structure curricula to help teachers inspire students through creativity. To my amazement he said, "Inspiration: isn't that a bit idealistic? Creativity can happen later."

Given these attitudes in the organizations that are setting the curricula, it's not surprising that many individual teachers are cautious about providing opportunities for students to be creative. This is a shame, because it means that student who are creative and energetic, but are interested in areas other than art or writing, often have no creative outlet other than trouble making, and fail to realize the creative opportunities open to them in the wider world.

I once ran an "Insight into Industry" exercise for a group of 130 13-year-olds in a tough inner-city comprehensive school. This was a well-designed exercise from the UK's Careers Research and Advisory Council,[24] in which teams of young people had to design and build a car from a kit of simple parts, and power it by their choice of elastic bands. We then raced the cars up an inclined ramp to see whose went furthest. One team was led by a lad, Barry, who was clearly very creative, always coming up to me to ask if some bright idea was permitted by the rules. To the visible amazement of the teachers, his team won. Their car went more than twice as far as the next best.

I pointed out to his teachers that he was clearly a born creative engineer who would do really well in any company's research and development department, but they found this hard to believe; he had such a reputation as a trouble maker that he was on the point of being excluded from school for the third time. They'd virtually given up on him.

I can well imagine that Barry was often a pain to teach, but I always hope that he remembered his moment of glory, and someone helped him channel his undoubted creativity in a productive direction.

The moral of this story is that if you think you aren't creative, or your kids are in trouble at school, ask yourself whether this is just because the environment doesn't offer the right creative outlet. It may or may not be possible to do anything about it at the time, but never let them grind down your creative self-confidence.

The myth of the Eureka Moment

The final common reason for a lack of creative self-confidence is the belief that if you are truly creative your ideas will arrive fully formed in a flash of inspiration. I call this the "myth of the Eureka Moment".

For many people, the story of Archimedes's flash of creative inspiration epitomizes the creative process.

Archimedes was born in about 285 BC and mainly lived in Syracuse on the eastern coast of Sicily. He is believed to have been close to Hieron II, King of Syracuse, who tried to encourage him to use his extraordinary talents for practical purposes. The king had commissioned a gold wreath to consecrate to the gods. When the wreath was delivered, it weighed the correct amount for which he had been charged. However, the king was suspicious that he might have been cheated, with some of the gold replaced by an equal weight of a cheaper metal such as silver or lead. Archimedes was pondering this while he had a bath, and suddenly realized that the water he displaced by getting into the bath was equal to his own volume. If he put the wreath in a full bowl of water, he could measure how much overflowed and this would give him the volume. He could then weigh the wreath and calculate the density; the ratio of the weight to the volume. If this was not the same as the density of gold, the wreath was a fake. The story goes that he was so excited by this that he jumped out of the bath naked and ran through the palace shouting "Eureka!" (Greek for "I have found it"). When Archimedes subsequently did the measurements he found that Hieron had indeed been cheated.

Archimedes was a real historical figure[25] and, whether or not the story is strictly true, it's a nice illustration of the intensity of the flash of creative insight that we experience when we have a creative idea.

The problem is that people take this too far and assume that truly creative people have ideas that emerge fully formed and perfect. If you believe this myth it's easy to think that you can't be truly creative if yours don't. This then damages your creative self-confidence.

The reality is that even very creative people expect to have repeated flashes of inspiration while they are developing their ideas. These flashes are interspersed with periods in which they are verifying their insight and uncovering its shortcomings, then preparing and incubating the next step. It is this process, the repeated cycles of preparation, incubation, illumination and verification, that takes the idea forward. If the idea is an important and radically new one, this process can take a long time.

The inventor James Dyson spent five years working on his ideas for a bagless vacuum cleaner, building and testing over 5,000 variants before he had one that he was satisfied with.

Similarly, Einstein spent ten years working on his theory of relativity from the time he posed his first thought experiment, at the age of 16, about what it would be like riding on a beam of light. While still at school, he'd realized that two pillars of physics, Newton and Maxwell, could not both be right about what a light beam would look like if one was travelling at the speed of light. He said later, "The germ of the special relativity theory was already present in that paradox."

He struggled with the paradox for a decade. In May 1905, exhausted and depressed, he was on the point of giving up. He later remembered riding in a streetcar in Bern and looking back at the famous clock tower that dominated the city. He then imagined what would happen if his streetcar raced away from the clock tower at the speed of light. He quickly realized that the clock would appear stopped, since light could not catch up to the streetcar, but his own clock in the streetcar would beat normally.

Then it suddenly hit him, the key to the entire problem. Einstein recalled, "A storm broke loose in my mind."

The answer was simple and elegant: time can beat at different rates throughout the universe, depending on how fast you move.[26] This was the famous flash of inspiration that resolved the paradox and became the theory of special relativity.

It had taken him ten years: persistence is a very important creative attribute.

Creative people are not immune from the myth of the Eureka Moment either. Mozart liked to give the impression that his compositions arrived fully formed, but he frequently complained of writer's block and made many revisions to his manuscripts.

In reality innovation tends to involve a lot of false starts and confusion, and ideas need to be "morphed" until they work. It's only in retrospect that the story is tidied up so that it sounds nice and logical.

"The myth of the Eureka Moment" is also unhelpful because it encourages you to feel that your first idea must be the ultimate and perfect solution. This then encourages you to try to bulldoze the idea through all objections and to ignore even helpful suggestions for how to improve the idea. As many of these objections and suggestions will have been soundly based, by ignoring them you are just reducing your chances of success.

Manuscript page from the score of Mozart's *Don Giovanni* (1787), showing the composer's extensive revisions
akg-london

Finally, if you succeed in getting to the stage of trying to implement the idea, the people who have been bulldozed and ignored will line up to block the idea. If you have been irritating enough, they will do this even if the idea is a good one and logically it would be in their best interests to support it.

The characteristics of creative people

When I was 16 and faced with the problem of choosing a university course which would then possibly decide my future career, a friend of mine suggested that I should meet her father, Gordon Glegg, a technical consultant, professional inventor and Cambridge University lecturer. His description of the wacky and interesting problems he'd had to solve sounded so fascinating I decided on the spot that I wanted to become the same – a consultant and professional inventor.

I now realize that I only had a fairly tenuous idea of what this involved, and it was distinctly influenced by the Heath Robinson cartoons of "Professor Branestawm" (like the one at the start of this chapter) that I'd enjoyed as a child.

I wasn't keen on the mad inventor hairstyle, but, without really thinking about it, I assumed that if I was to be a great inventor I needed to be disorganized and messy. I took pride in having a messy desk, overflowing with ideas and samples, with balls of crumpled paper all around it.

It was only several years later that I began to realize that I could develop an idea much more effectively if I could find the work I'd done on it the day before. Being organized would help my creativity, not hinder it.

I'm still incredulous about people who can live in minimalist homes without filling them up with interesting things (other people would call it clutter), but when I'm developing ideas I am rigorous about documenting them as they progress, trying to "lock down" where I've got to when I take a break. This allows me to incubate ideas for improvements while I'm doing something else, and then resume from where I've left off.

David Armstrong, an organizational psychologist at the Tavistock Consultancy Service,[27] points out that creativity is associated with a feeling of "freedom within a secure framework". If, as small children, we know that our parents love us and there are consistent rules about what is and is not permitted, we feel free to play and our creativity can develop. If, on the other hand, we feel uncertain about the circumstances in which we will be rewarded or punished, we become fearful and unable to be creative.

The product development staff at one client of mine told me that their top management had told them to "be innovative or you'll be fired". They very much wanted to respond, but as no one was clear what "be innovative" really meant, or what one had to do to avoid being fired, their flurry of activity was remarkably unproductive.

As creative adults, we can help our creativity by cultivating that same sense of freedom within a secure framework. The framework keeps us focused on our objective and helps us avoid solutions that won't work, so for an engineer the framework would include the rules of physics; engineering doesn't work without obeying the laws of physics. A musical composer will use their knowledge of harmony to create the effect they want.

A secure framework helps us focus our efforts, but does not necessarily mean an absence of stress. Creative people are often very driven, and Beethoven created many of his greatest works while in financial difficulties.

Misconceptions about the creative personality are common, but successful creative people do have certain common personality traits: they tend to have a personality type that's comfortable with intuition and openness, but as we will see later, they also tend to be quite complex people.

Personality and intuition

Creative people tend to be comfortable with using hunches and intuition. They also tend to be comfortable with keeping things open and flexible, considering alternative options and delaying the final decisions. For other, less creative people, the ambiguity and uncertainty of this often feels unbearable so they jump too quickly to the "obvious" solution, thus missing the opportunity to unearth something better and more creative.

One of the highest profile examples of the power of intuition came in 1986, when the *Challenger* space shuttle blew up 73 seconds after lift off, killing all seven crewmembers and setting back the NASA space programme for over two years.

It was particularly tragic because the engineers at the booster rocket manufacturers, Morton Thiokol, had tried to stop the launch in a four-hour teleconference with NASA the night before. The engineers' concern was that the O-ring seals on the booster rockets wouldn't function properly at the low launch temperatures that were expected. They tried as hard as they could to persuade NASA of the danger and get them to abort the launch, but the problem was that they couldn't prove their hunch; it's understandably tricky to test fire a 56m-long space shuttle booster rocket at – 5°C. This meant that although there was a lot of data, at the time it seemed inconclusive.

The culture in NASA and Morton Thiokol meant that intuitions don't get much of a look in. As NASA rocket specialist Judson Lovingood said during the subsequent investigations, "If you say, 'hey, I've got a funny feeling this thing's going to blow', they'll take you to the funny farm."[28] The explosion was especially sad because, although at the time the engineers couldn't justify their intuition, it subsequently turned out that it was correctly pointing them to the pattern hidden in their data. As we'll see in Chapter 7, they already had all the data they needed, if only they could have articulated it in a way that would have convinced NASA.

In this case the intuition was proved right. This isn't always true, of course, though research shows that experts are very often right about their hunches, so long as these relate to their domain of knowledge. On the other hand, novices' hunches are very often wrong.

Some of the most thorough research on the relationship between creative performance and personality has been carried out using a personality assessment method known as the Myers-Briggs Type Indicator® or MBTI® instrument.[29]

This is based on a theory of personality developed by the great Swiss psychologist Carl Jung (1875–1961), which was then developed by his contemporary Katharine Cook Briggs and her daughter Isabel Briggs Myers who wanted to understand people around them. Their work on the MBTI test was particularly stimulated by the waste of human potential they saw in the Second World War, when people were often placed in jobs that were very poorly matched with their personalities.

The MBTI test is now probably the most widely used personality test, with over two million administered each year in the US alone, mostly for personal awareness training, leadership development, team understanding and conflict reduction.

The MBTI test is based on Jung's observation that individuals have a tendency to direct their energy and attention inwardly, referred to as "introversion" (I), or externally, referred to as "extraversion" (E). When we are mentally active we deal with the outer world either by taking in information, referred to as "Perceiving" (P), or organizing it, referred to as "Judging" (J). He identified two different ways in which we perceive: in the MBTI test these are known as "Sensing", given the letter S, or "Intuition", given the letter N. The two ways of Judging are either "Thinking" (T) or "Feeling" (F). These preferences can then be combined to give 16 dominant personality types, each given a four-letter code such as ENTP or ISFJ.

Two aspects of the MBTI personality type are particularly interesting when exploring creativity and the adoption of ideas:

Sensing (S) – Intuition (N)
Judging (J) – Perceiving (P)

The "Self Assessment of Your Type" box will show where you fit on these, and explore what it means for your potential strengths and problem areas.

About 75% of the general US population are Sensing types (S), tending to be comfortable with their past experience, and liking concrete information and facts. The Intuitive types (N) prefer to trust their inspiration, and prefer to look at connections and the big picture. They are in a minority, which perhaps explains the emphasis given to targets, metrics and data in political and organizational life.

Professions and organizations tend to attract people with the appropriate personality type, so about 90% of artists[30] are Intuitive types (N), while about 80% of accountants are Sensing types (S). When one personality type predominates in a group, this has a profound impact on its "feel" as people adapt their behaviour to fit in, which helps to explain why some groups of people stimulate our creativity, while others feel dry and draining.

Self-Assessment of Your Type[31]

Although you can only get an accurate assessment of your MBTI type by taking the actual MBTI questionnaire and having feedback from an accredited professional, you should be able to make a reasonable self-assessment of your preferences by considering which of the descriptions seems to give the best fit to your natural personality. The authors of the MBTI® instrument actually recommend that you start by doing this, and then, if the questionnaire suggests a different type, use the feedback for whichever seems more useful to you.

Note that your natural personality is the way you are when you are feeling comfortable and relaxed, and not under pressure to perform a role.

The first aspect that is particularly important for creativity is

S-N: How do you prefer to take in information?

People who prefer Sensing like to take in information that is real and tangible – what is actually happening. They are observant about the specifics of what is going on around them, and are especially attuned to practical realities.

People who prefer Intuition like to take in information by seeing the big picture, focusing on the relationships and connections between facts. They want to grasp patterns and are especially attuned to seeing new possibilities.

Sensing (S) characteristics	Intuition (N) characteristics
■ Oriented to practical, present realities.	■ Oriented to future possibilities.
■ Factual and concrete.	■ Imaginative, verbally creative.
■ Focus on what is real and actual.	■ Focus on patterns and meanings in data.
■ Observe and remember specifics.	■ Remember specifics when they relate to a pattern.
■ Build carefully and thoroughly towards conclusions.	■ Move quickly to conclusions, follow hunches.
■ Understand ideas though practical application.	■ Want to clarify ideas and theories before putting them into practice.
■ Trust experience.	■ Trust inspiration.

The second important aspect is

J-P: How do you deal with the outer world?

People who prefer to use their Judging process in the outer world like to live in a planned, orderly way, seeking to regulate and manage their lives. They want to make decisions, come to closure and move on. Their lives tend to be structured and organized, and they like to have things settled. Sticking to a plan and schedule is very important to them, and they are energized by getting things done.

People who prefer to use their Perceiving process in the outer world like to live in a flexible, spontaneous way, seeking to experience and understand life, rather than control it. Detailed plans and final decisions feel confining to them; they prefer to stay open to new information and last-minute options. They are energized by their resourcefulness in adapting to the demands of the moment.

Judging (J) characteristics	Perceiving (P) characteristics
■ Scheduled.	■ Spontaneous.
■ Organize their lives.	■ Flexible.
■ Systematic.	■ Casual.
■ Methodical.	■ Open-ended.
■ Make short and long term plans.	■ Adapt, change course.
■ Like to have things decided.	■ Like things loose and open to change.
■ Try to avoid last-minute stresses.	■ Feel energized by last-minute pressures.

By considering these two tables, you should be able to decide which group you fall into: NP, NJ, SP or SJ.

If you find it hard to decide one of the letters, this may mean that you don't have a very strong preference on this aspect. Completing the full MBTI questionnaire can often help give you more insight into your preferences.

Interestingly, although people at junior levels in many large western organizations may feel that they are being driven to behave like S types, the proportion of N types increases as one rises through the ranks of most companies. Typically, 50% of top management are N types, double the population average, and the proportion is often even higher in the most creative organizations. This is because senior executives have to focus on the big picture, need vision and tend to have to make complex decisions on inadequate data. Following hunches (which are of course based on the person's cumulative past experience) is often the only way forward. This means that if you want to get on at work, it's important not to neglect the intuitive aspects of your personality, even if the culture seems to discourage it.

The distribution of MBTI types seems to be fairly similar round the world, although the popularity of psychometric testing differs in different cultures. However, there can be quite significant cultural differences in which MBTI types get promoted within organizations in different cultures. An Intuitive N type is even more likely to be promoted to become a senior executive in Japan than in the USA, for example, reflecting the much greater acceptance of the use of intuition in Japanese corporations.

A few years ago, I was on a European Union study tour of Japan, looking at how major Japanese companies did product innovation. I asked the senior managers we were meeting how they decided which products to develop in the early stages of the innovation process: did they use intuition or market research? Whereas senior managers in most British or American corporations would have been embarrassed to have admitted to a group of important foreign visitors that they used intuition, their Japanese counterparts firmly said, "intuition is far more important than market research".[32]

Studies have also shown that the Intuitive N types are more likely to be creative than the S types.[33] Some of the earliest work on this was carried out at the Institute for Personality Assessment and Research (IPAR). They compared people working in a variety of creative fields, such as architecture, with the general public. They also asked people working in those creative fields to pick out the most creative of their peers. They then measured their MBTI personality type and found that these highly creative people were virtually all N types, a far, far greater proportion than could have happened by chance.[34]

The combined results of 20 years' research at the IPAR showed that someone's preference for using Intuition (N) rather than Sensing (S) was the most significant aspect of their personality in predicting their creativity. It was three times more important than the next most significant factor, their preference for Perceiving (P) (keeping things open and flexible) rather than Judging (J) (making decisions and plans).

Another study on the impact of personality was carried out by the business development specialists, Greg Stevens and James Burley, who looked at 267 projects in a large chemicals multinational run by 69 different project leaders over a ten-year period.[35] This study showed that teams run by project leaders with the most creative personality characteristics made 13 times more money for the company than those run by less creative leaders. As predicted by the IPAR research, comfort with intuition was the most important personality characteristic in predicting whether an individual would be so much more productive than the others.

These personality traits are fairly stable but are not immutably fixed. We can make a significant difference by paying attention to neglected areas and practising behaviour patterns that may initially feel uncomfortable, but which help us be more effective in achieving our aims.

Sometimes we find we operate in quite different ways in different environments, so for example, one half-Italian engineer at a large aero-engine manufacturer told me that he behaved like an S in the systematic atmosphere at work, but was an N when at home with his family and Italian relatives. He had clearly developed the flexibility to succeed in both environments, even though the N style felt more comfortable and natural to him.

Personality preferences can also evolve naturally as we develop. For example, as people reach their mid to late 30s some of the more neglected personality characteristics can start to appear.[36] Some people seem to be more open to this process of development than others, but if it is resisted it can lead to the typical "midlife crisis". For example, people whose MBTI results suggest that they are an S will tend to trust their experience and the facts, rather than intuition. However, one typical midlife change is the emergence of hunches. This has been described as feeling "unsettling, weird but interesting".[37]

If this change happens to you, it is very powerful to listen to your hunch, then research it thoroughly to gather the information you need to feel comfortable and see if it is right. If you are lucky, you will find that very often your hunch will be pointing you in a useful direction and you will start to get the confidence to develop this more neglected side of your personality.

It can help your intuition emerge if you deliberately give it space to do so. After learning about this, one Sensing-Judging (SJ) manager in her mid 30s said to me, "On the tough items, I put them into a parking lot for my drive home. I drive about one hour each way to work and it is amazing to me how

I can resolve things so much more quickly in that period than when I am beating on them at work."

It is important to realize that if you have a strongly Intuitive personality type (N) you have the potential to be very creative, but it's not guaranteed. You can also be so dysfunctional that you achieve far less with your creativity than someone who is a Sensing type (S).

The way in which your creativity expresses itself is influenced by all your personality characteristics, so your preference for Judging (J) or Perceiving (P) influences the way your preference for Sensing (S) or Intuition (N) is expressed. Together they help determine your potential strengths and weaknesses. Your ability to make the best of these plays a large part in determining how successful you will be.

For example, if your self-assessment suggests that you are an NP, you may be highly creative, producing a wealth of ideas. People with NP preference often dislike following rules and processes, so you may be thought of a "Creative Maverick",[38] difficult to corral, but valuable. However, if circumstances have not been helpful to you, or if you have not had the opportunity to develop your weaker areas, the same basic personality preferences could lead you to become a "Scatterbrain", continually bouncing from one idea to another and never completing anything.

The other combinations, NJ, SP and SJ, all also have their particular strengths and potential problem areas. Having worked out these two aspects of your MBTI personality type using the self assessment exercise above, you can use the chart on pages 44–51 to explore how people are likely to see you.

Are you a Creative Maverick, or a Scatterbrain?

Are you a Visionary Leader, or a Fixated Bore?

Are you an Innovative Trouble-Shooter, or a Mad Inventor?

Are you a Careful Conservator, or an Obsessive Nitpicker?

Understanding your own personality and the characteristics of others helps you be more effective. For example, the Careful Conservators and Creative Mavericks often get very frustrated with each other, because the Careful Conservators refuse to go along with the enthusiastic hunches of the Creative Mavericks until they have enough data to feel comfortable that the idea is sound. To a Creative Maverick, this just makes them feel as if the Careful Conservator is being negative and stalling, so they will often try to overcome it by making the idea sound more and more exciting, and being more exaggerated in their enthusiasm. Unfortunately, however, this just makes the Careful Conservator feel more and more worried that the idea is risky and poorly thought through.

On the other hand, if a Careful Conservator and a Creative Maverick can develop the mutual respect and understanding to work together, the combination can be very effective, because each thrives doing the bits the other one hates.

Once you realize that different people will need different things to feel comfortable with your idea, it's also much easier to provide it to them.

Complexity

Although the Creative Maverick personality type tends to be very highly represented amongst creative people, each personality type has its potential problem areas. None is a panacea for greatness and all types are valuable in their own ways.

The leading American psychologist Mihaly Csikszentmihalyi studies creativity, happiness and the sense of well-being. He is probably best known for his work on the concept of "Flow": a zen-like state of total oneness with the task. He describes it as "being completely involved in an activity for its own sake. The ego falls away. Time flies. Every action, movement, and thought follows inevitably from the previous one, like playing jazz. Your whole being is involved, and you're using your skills to the utmost."[39]

He points out that one of the most significant personality traits of successful creative people is their own complexity.[40] They show contradictory personality traits simultaneously, whereas most people tend to show one or the other, but not both.

These traits are not merged into a bland average, but can both be exhibited strongly. It is noticeable that the most successful creative people have the flexibility to move from one to the other in quick succession as the occasion demands.

Energetic and yet contemplative

Making a significant creative advance is difficult. It doesn't happen in a single "Eureka Moment". This means that successful creative individuals tend to have the ability to focus intently and energetically for long periods on the subject that interests them.

Creative Maverick or Scatterbrain?

If your self-assessment suggests you are an NP, you may well find this page useful. A high proportion of the most creative people are NPs.

At your best

You are highly creative, producing a wealth of creative ideas, and exploring them enthusiastically and energetically.

You will probably tend to hate routine and imposed process, but will tackle tasks energetically and unconventionally once you get interested in them.

You may well have a powerful intuitive sense of a vision, feel very passionate about it and be excited by all the alternatives.

You see connections and possibilities that others miss.

Things to try

Potential problem areas

You bounce from idea to idea, never committing enough energy on one to make it real, because you can't decide between them.

You love bouncing around, gathering new information and ideas. However, your decision-making will tend to be a quiet inner process. If you find it hard to settle on which idea to go with, it can be very useful to take the time to write a summary of the rationale for the competing ideas, together with their advantages and disadvantages, then sit down privately to reflect on them and make your decision.

Your passion is inspiring, but other people can find you surprisingly hard to understand. It often helps a lot to slow down and take the time to plan and structure what you want to say in advance so that you can make sure you get your key messages across in the right order, even it feels to you as if this makes your idea boring.

If you are too absorbed in your intuition and the inner world of your ideas, you may not have paid enough attention to why your ideas are needed, or to inconvenient reality. This can make it hard for you to engage others; particularly the very grounded people who will want to know why your idea is needed and to feel confident that it will be practical before they can commit themselves.

| Organize yourself. | Slow down. | Ground your ideas in reality. |

Visionary Leader[41] or Fixated Bore?

If your self-assessment suggests that you are an NJ you may well find this page useful. NJs are the best represented group amongst senior executives.

At your best

You combine vision with decisiveness.

You are likely to be curious, creative and visionary, but in a quieter, more private way than the Creative Mavericks. You will tend to develop an idea internally and privately, perhaps for quite a long time, before sharing it with anyone.

You will probably be quite happy fitting in with the rules and defined processes and will like making decisions.

You can be very good at coming up with creative and visionary solutions to complex problems, if you are given time and space to do so.

You will probably need quiet space in order to allow your intuition time to work. If you are in an environment where this is hard to find, it can be really valuable to make a deliberate effort to create space for it, for example during the drive to work or while walking the dog.

Things to try

Potential problem areas

You may well have a strong inner drive to make decisions and get closure and this can mean that you don't give yourself long enough to think about the idea. You then make idiosyncratic or changeable decisions.

If this tends to happen, it may well be valuable to choose a few trusted people with whom you can discuss your embryonic ideas at an earlier stage than would normally feel comfortable to you.

Because your intuition is a private process, you may spend far too long refining your idea privately, only sharing it when it seems obvious to you and ready to implement. Unfortunately, it may well not be at all obvious to others, so it may then be very frustrating to find that you have to do a lot of explanation and persuasion before they will do anything to help.

If your idea is resisted, your decisiveness and the strength of your inner vision can then make you very single minded and dictatorial about your idea. This can then very easily become a vicious circle, as you become ever more fixated and critical of your opposition, which makes your opposition even less likely to adopt your idea or even to debate with you. If this is the case, it can be very helpful when you realize the impact your actions are having, and start using a broader range of techniques for getting people engaged in your ideas.

Share your embryonic ideas.

Give yourself space.

Cultivate your flexibility.

Innovative Trouble-Shooter or Mad Inventor?

If your self-assessment suggests you are an SP, you may well find this page useful. A high proportion of amateur inventors are SPs.

At your best

You will tend to have an active, hands-on approach to life. You will like variety and take action resourcefully to fix problems and get things done. You will tend to like doing things, rather than endlessly talking about doing things.

Your style of creativity will tend to be practical and realistic, adaptive rather than radically innovative. You will tend to build your ideas based on your own experience of the world around you, and the facts as you perceive them.

You can be very good at coming up with innovative solutions to real needs, particularly if you are introverted and thoughtful.

If you are extroverted, people will often find you gregarious and fun to be with.

Things to try

Potential problem areas

You may get so caught up in the world around you that you don't take the time you need to think your ideas through and evaluate them. This then means that you may find it difficult to make decisions, and so postpone them or make them haphazardly in response to the immediate perceived needs.

You may invent a niche product or a solution to a problem facing you, failing to see that even though the idea meets your needs, it will be of no interest to anyone else.

It's important to ensure that the information on which you are basing your ideas is as valid as you think, otherwise you may find others reject your ideas as impractical or that you have imposed unnecessary constraints on your creativity.

If you don't feel appreciated enough for what you can offer, you may focus entirely on excitement or become overly impulsive and hence find it difficult to achieve.

Question your assumed constraints.

Think about others' requirements.

Gather new information and experiences.

Careful Conservator or Obstructive Nitpicker?

If your self-assessment suggests you are an SJ, you may well find this page useful. A high proportion of accountants are SJs.

At your best

You will tend to be thorough, precise and realistic, liking to work in a well-organized, well-defined process. You like dealing with detail and getting it right.

Once you are convinced a change is needed you can be very energetic in devising solutions.

You are firmly grounded in reality and past experience.

Things to try

Potential problem areas

You will need to be convinced that the proposed change is needed and that it will lead to something better than the status quo, before you will drop well-proven ways of working. You tend to take more convincing than some of the other groups because you like to do things thoroughly, so you know that change will involve you in a lot of work.

You may be particularly likely to say "we tried that years ago and it didn't work". People may well see you as change resistant, without realizing that it's probably more a resistance to being changed, which is a typical reaction for anyone.

If you are logically minded you are particularly vulnerable to seeing the world in black or white, rather than shades of grey: if a piece of information doesn't fit with your view of the world you are likely either to ignore or reject it. This can be a major handicap to your creativity.

Give others space to do it "their" way.

Gather new information and experiences.

Learning new creativity tools, techniques and processes will tend to help your creativity.

It's important not to be always "on", because the creative process needs to alternate periods when you are energetically gathering information or thinking analytically with periods of quieter reflection to incubate ideas and listen to your intuition. The incubation state is a relatively low arousal state, in which the mind is at rest but intently focused. One artist described this state of mind to me as "expectant, persistent and divergent".

Creative people will often deliberately go into this, and develop their own ways of promoting it. The state very often happens when one's body is engaged in a relatively routine task, like driving, walking the dog, decorating or simple DIY. This maybe explains why the power tool manufacturer Robert Bosch gets sent six ideas a week (or so the engineers told me) for devices to hold power drills at right angles to a wall, even though they already have such a device in their catalogue.

The transition between wakefulness and sleep is also a very productive time for this incubation. Many great creative individuals deliberately use the hypnagogic state (falling asleep) and hypnopompic state (waking from sleep) to generate ideas.

Thomas Edison was the inventor of the first practical electric light bulb and possibly the world's most prolific inventor, with over 1,093 patents. To access the hypnagogic state he would sit on a chair which was placed on a sheet of steel, holding two steel balls in his hand. He would focus intently on the need for an idea and allow himself to drift off to sleep. As this happened, his hands would let go of the balls and they would fall on the steel sheet and wake him up. He would then write down the ideas that occurred to him. It is said that the surrealist painter, Salvador Dali, used to tap into the same state, balancing his chin on the end of a spoon, propped up on the table. Once again, when he started to fall asleep he would be woken up and would sketch his ideas.[42]

This state is very productive. This is because when we are dreaming we make strange associations and connections between things, probably as part of the process of learning and memory. It can very often produce new creative insights, but normally the chemical noradrenaline is produced to stop us remembering them and getting confused with reality. In the hypnagogic and hypnopompic state, however, we are still dreaming, but the brain has stopped producing noradrenaline so we can remember the results.

When I'm running courses I find about 50% of people report that they regularly find they wake from sleep with useful creative ideas, even without going to the lengths of Edison and Dali. I find this very useful myself, and suspect many more could do it if they tried.

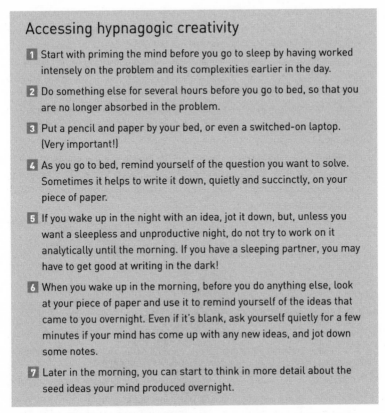

Accessing hypnagogic creativity

1 Start with priming the mind before you go to sleep by having worked intensely on the problem and its complexities earlier in the day.

2 Do something else for several hours before you go to bed, so that you are no longer absorbed in the problem.

3 Put a pencil and paper by your bed, or even a switched-on laptop. (Very important!)

4 As you go to bed, remind yourself of the question you want to solve. Sometimes it helps to write it down, quietly and succinctly, on your piece of paper.

5 If you wake up in the night with an idea, jot it down, but, unless you want a sleepless and unproductive night, do not try to work on it analytically until the morning. If you have a sleeping partner, you may have to get good at writing in the dark!

6 When you wake up in the morning, before you do anything else, look at your piece of paper and use it to remind yourself of the ideas that came to you overnight. Even if it's blank, ask yourself quietly for a few minutes if your mind has come up with any new ideas, and jot down some notes.

7 Later in the morning, you can start to think in more detail about the seed ideas your mind produced overnight.

Playful and yet realistic

Successful creative individuals also succeed in combining playfulness, fantasy and naivety with discipline and attention to reality.

They talk about "playing with ideas" and "kicking ideas around" or refer to the prototypes of their inventions as "toys". They use metaphor or imagine the impossible as an intermediate step for generating a practical idea. Creative brainstorm sessions may well be accompanied by gales of laughter.

These habits can all be very worrying to less creative people, who assume that the playfulness means that their creative colleagues are not taking the problem seriously enough. It can also create jealousy and envy if people think that the "Creatives" are having more fun than they are themselves. However, the reality is that creativity works best when playfulness is combined with a disciplined attention to reality.

The Harvard University social psychologist Professor Teresa Amabile defines a creative solution as one that is novel, but also "appropriate" for its purpose.[43] It will be original, not just bizarre. The random splashes of paint that fall on the floor while one is decorating might form a novel pattern, but one would not call them "creative". However, the action paintings by the artist Jackson Pollock (1912–56) hang in the US National Gallery of Art in Washington DC and other top galleries around the world. In 2006 his picture *No. 5, 1948* was sold for $140 million to a Mexican financier and became the most expensive picture ever sold by any artist.

Pollock's pictures are renowned for their creativity because although the patterns may seem superficially random, they were produced with great intent and somehow this shines through. Nicolas Pioch described the way Pollock worked thus: "He danced in semi-ecstasy over canvases spread across the floor, lost in his patternings, dripping and dribbling with total control."[44]

One's ideas may well start with a flight of fancy, but to be successful they need also to become grounded in reality. The painter must know how paint behaves. The engineer must understand the limitations imposed by the laws of physics. As Gordon Glegg, the consultant and inventor who set me off on my career, used to tell his Cambridge University engineering students, "It's important to know the difference between an impossible impossibility, and something that is just impossible."

If it was "just" impossible, he encouraged us to give it a go. I've always found this really helpful advice.

It can be very helpful to start the process of looking for an idea by removing some (but not all) of the constraints, but not at random. It is the depth of experience in a domain that gives the expert the wisdom to know which constraints to relax temporarily to release a creative idea, and which to maintain.

Passionate and yet objective

Most creative people are very passionate about their work because otherwise it would be hard to maintain their interest and enthusiasm for it. Nevertheless, it is also important to be objective and detached in order to produce good work. This creates a conflict between the passionate desire for excellence and the internal critic that says "the idea is not good enough yet". Successful creative people are able to sustain this tension for long periods, and often use it to drive themselves on.

The openness, sensitivity and passion of creative people often make criticism and rejection very painful. Inevitably there will be a lot of this when they are exposed and isolated proposing a new idea. However, there is also the huge pleasure of the creative process, and the satisfaction of feeling that your ideas are making a difference.

Independent and yet connected

Successful creative people are able to combine a fierce independence with the ability to understand and relate to other people in the domain they are working in. It is important to be comfortable being alone, because one usually needs to be alone to write, to do experiments or to pursue new and different ideas. As we'll see later, if one is too closely immersed in a group, "group think" will make it very difficult to think of radically new ideas. There will also be too much going on to juggle the complexities and ambiguities of a half-formed idea. However, the loner in the shed is also very unlikely to be successful. Good ideas need to be built on the existing body of knowledge and to connect with it; otherwise they will either be irrelevant or will turn out just to have been a reinvention of the wheel.

The connection with others also helps build the ideas. Csikszentmihalyi quotes the artist Nina Holton describing the role of sociability in art: "You can't really work entirely alone in your place. You want to have a fellow artist come over and talk things over with you. 'How does that strike you?' You have to have some sort of feedback."

Creative people, at their best, are also very open to new information and ideas and more tolerant of risk than others. This means that when there's a problem they are often much more willing to accept that it exists than are less creative people, but also much more likely to be driven to try to solve it.

They will also often combine self-confidence, pride and even aggression with humbleness and a willingness to subordinate their own personal comfort and advancement to the success of their project. It is difficult to advance new ideas, so you need to be clear and strong for your idea, not swamped by the way things have always been done in the past. However, ideas are always related to other ideas, and it is the awareness of this that leads to modesty and a willingness to let go when the time is right. As we will see later, this selfless, modest attitude makes it much more likely that people will accept an idea, rather than if it is promoted in an aggressive, combative way.

Creative people will often say that they have been lucky to have been in the right place at the right time, and to have spotted an opportunity.[45] Others will point out that it is your attitude, preparation and courage that will make your luck.

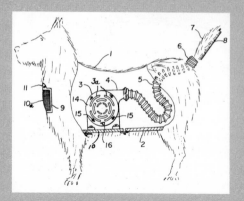

Engaging with reality

CREATIVITY IS GREAT FUN, but as we saw in the first chapter, it's tough to win through and produce something that really makes a difference.

Part of the problem is that as creative people we can be quite impossible. As we saw in the discussion about personality in the previous chapter, all too often we bounce from idea to idea, never settling on one or the other, or we get utterly fixated and single-minded about our great idea, insisting that it's accepted in its entirety. Alternatively, we may be so inspired by our vision that we ignore the practical details about why it's needed or how to make it work.

Then when people fail to get interested in it, we get all upset.

The Careful Conservator types can be very irritating when they insist on demanding to know why the idea is needed before they will do anything other than just keep picking holes in it, or complaining that we're not being systematic in how we develop it. However, they do actually have a point: we have a much better chance of coming up with ideas that will get adopted and make a difference if we are clear about the focus of our work and realistic about the constraints.

This doesn't mean to say that we should stop having fun, being visionary, or playing with impossibilities, but just that ideas are so important that the process of developing them deserves to be taken seriously too, whether we have an idea for a better mousetrap, for fighting world poverty, or for a fulfilling way of spending our time in retirement.

This chapter discusses some of the key principles for developing ideas that will have a reasonable chance of getting adopted.

Focus on your objective

I was once developing a workshop with the eminent artist Maurice Cockrill RA, and we came up with a phrase to describe the creative process that we both used to develop creative ideas. In my case they were new products, in his they were works of art, but we both agreed that the key thing was to "Focus on the objective, and hold the space."

We both found this a very evocative and useful phase, because it encapsulates two key aspects of the creative process. You need to know where you are going if you are to have a hope of arriving, but if you are to be creative you also need to allow room for ambiguity, uncertainty and the unexpected.

A clear focus on our objectives is very important, but is surprisingly often neglected. As we saw in the last chapter, if someone just tells you to "be innovative or you will be fired", the brief is so vague that it's very hard to be productively creative. In contrast, in 2001, a group of major chemical and life-science companies, led by the pharmaceutical company Eli Lilly, set up a website[46] on which they posted "challenges", inviting scientists to compete to solve them for a prize of up to $100,000. Since then, a steady stream of scientists from around the world have solved the challenges and received their rewards, while the companies have had their problems solved for much less than it would have cost them internally.

Find the unmet need

Your idea is only likely to make a difference if it's needed. This is why the Holy Grail for companies, professional inventors and campaigners is to find and solve the "unmet need".

Finding a good unmet need increases the chance that you will succeed in getting your idea adopted, but the sense of satisfaction of solving even relatively trivial needs helps motivate your creativity.

I had to admit that the results of my labours on developing my gourmet toaster, mentioned in Chapter 1, probably weren't really going to make the world a better place. Starvation, poverty and the destruction of our natural environment were probably going to continue unaffected by my work, and might even be made worse. Nevertheless, I had fun developing it, learned a lot, earned my salary and played my part in making the world's economy function. It felt good thinking of all the money the company would make, and all the people who'd have nicer breakfasts if it worked.

The glow of satisfaction shines even more brightly, however, if you feel that you're really working on something worthwhile. This is why many charities find that they can attract good staff while quite openly paying them 10% or so below the normal "non-charitable" rate for the job. At the opposite extreme, companies in sectors like nuclear power or the petrochemical industry find it hard to attract the best graduates, so have to put a lot of effort into recruitment and have to pay significantly above average to compensate for the feel-bad factor.

Finding a good unmet need is surprisingly hard. Some unmet needs are obvious, but solving them is often an "impossible impossibility". Doubling your take-home pay overnight (legally), eliminating world hunger, or persuading your teenagers to keep their rooms tidy all probably fall into this category. Non-obvious unmet needs are trickier to spot, but potentially much more valuable if you can do so.

One example is SMS texting. Although a few people had a hunch that the ability to send messages to a mobile phone might be useful, no one foresaw its success. There was no single inventor of SMS; rather, it came about from the unwitting collaboration of several different groups: in this case, a multinational industrial standards committee, engineers trying to simplify their lives and rebellious teenagers.

The ground for SMS was set in 1987 by one of the working parties that was setting the standards for GSM mobile phones (this became the standard mobile-phone system in Europe and much of the rest of the world). They had a hunch that it would be useful to combine the functions of a pager and a mobile phone, so they made sure the standards specified that it should be possible to send a short (160-character) text message to a mobile phone. They saw this as being used for commercial services; for example, to tell someone that they had a voice message, or tell a delivery driver where to go next, but didn't see much need for the recipient to be able to send a reply much longer than "OK".

The next stage came when engineers in various companies started designing GSM mobile phones. Some have told me that they designed their phones to be able to send messages of a reasonable length as well as receive them, just because they found they had a little spare space available and were looking for something useful to put in it. They did this purely selfishly, because they thought it would help them "debug" their early designs, rather than because they foresaw what was about to happen.

To the industry's great surprise, teenagers started using SMS to send messages themselves. This probably started with the internet chat room culture, which was already around, where teenagers had been chatting to each other using shorthand and abbreviations. They "invented" the sort of "cu l8r" shorthand that then took off for texting, possibly because it was fun and cool to misspell words, maybe also because they weren't very good at spelling or typing.

This was the vital final element that made texting take off and, together with the subsequent invention of predictive texting, become the success it is today. By 2007, the industry estimated that five billion messages were being sent a day, accounting for a substantial chunk of most operators' revenues.

SMS was an unexpected success, but all too often we have completely unrealistic beliefs about how wonderful our idea is. This can be a problem for anyone, but people with some personality types are more vulnerable than others. As we saw in the last chapter, one common creative personality type is the Innovative Trouble-Shooter or Mad Inventor. If you are one, your strength is that you are focused on the needs that you perceive around you. Your risk area is that you can get too narrowly focused on an "unmet need" that only you need, and hence waste your efforts (at least if you were hoping that the world would beat a path to your door about it).

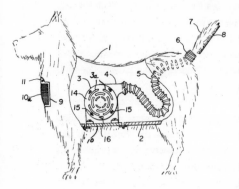

A vacuum cleaner disguised as a toy dog

Consider the invention of the Combined Toy Dog and Vacuum Cleaner, US Patent No. 3,771,192.

This is a patent for a vacuum cleaner which is disguised as a toy dog. The inventor's idea was that this "enables vacuum cleaning a dog after a haircut and grooming, without causing fear to the dog".

The inventor was unlikely to meet the world's most fundamental needs. Unfortunately, she was also unlikely even to cover her patent costs.

I suspect that she had fallen into the classic trap of assuming that the rest of the world wants what you want.

As social psychologists point out, we all have a tendency to overestimate how common our beliefs and opinions are.[47] This tendency is called the "false-consensus effect". In one experiment to demonstrate this, passers-by on the university campus were asked if they would walk around for half an hour wearing a sandwich board reading "Eat at Joe's". They were then asked their views on the proportion of other people who would make the same decision. In each case, whether they had agreed or refused, they thought about two thirds would choose to do the same.

Psychologists have various theories about why this happens. It may be because we are better at noticing and remembering information from people who are similar to us or who agree with us. It might also be because it could be logical to assume that others in the same situation as ourselves will come to the same decision that we did. Another group of explanations is about motivation and self-esteem. We feel better about ourselves if we believe that our opinions are common, because social consensus gives us a sense of social support and validation. We are therefore motivated to believe that others will think in the way that we do.

We also tend to overestimate how unique we are, and tend to assume that, on almost any scale from good to bad, we are nearer the "good" end of the spectrum. This is called the "false-uniqueness effect". Most drivers think they are better than average, even drivers who are in hospital after an accident. In a sample of Australian workers, 86% think they work better than average and only 1% think they are worse than average. The Australian social psychologists Martha Augoustinos and Iain Walker point out that this effect could well be driven by the same need for self-esteem as the false-consensus effect.

It seems that we like to think that our abilities are unique and our opinions common. This can badly mislead us when we are trying to decide whether the world will beat a path to our door to get our new invention.

How many people in the world use a vacuum cleaner on their dogs? There's obviously at least one person, but even if she's not alone, would disguising the vacuum cleaner as a dog actually make the dog any less scared of being vacuum cleaned? Out of curiosity I tried vacuum cleaning my head. It doesn't hurt, but certainly feels weird. Dogs may well be scared of the process, but I suspect it's more to do with the noise or the strange sucking feeling than the shape of the vacuum cleaner.

I suspect that the global market for combined toy dogs and vacuum cleaners is pretty small, although there's probably a much bigger market for ways to clean dogs. Companies spend millions on market research, but I often use a search engine like Google to get a quick feel for whether a topic is of global interest. Typing in "vacuuming dogs" gave 26 hits, of which most were facetious. Typing in "cleaning dogs" gave 6,772 hits, not that different to the 9,800 for "cleaning sinks". There are lots of sink-cleaning products around, so quite possibly there's space for a few products for cleaning dogs.

I suspect that she had also fallen into the trap of assuming that her first (and only?) idea for a solution was the best one. This is very seldom true, so she would have had a much better chance of using her creativity to make a difference if she had used her idea just as a pointer towards an unmet need: a problem that needed fixing, rather than a solution.

As we'll see later, she might more profitably have used her idea to define a question relating to a broader underlying unmet need: for example, "How can I groom a dog easily and cleanly?"

Asking questions like this will stimulate a variety of ideas. For example, one possible solution might well be to combine a vacuum cleaner with a toy dog, but alternatively one could start thinking about dog-cleaning attachments for an ordinary vacuum cleaner, ways of encouraging dogs to groom and clean themselves, better dog brushes or better ways to clean up after having groomed a dog. The ideas all tend to cross-fertilize one another, each one tending to address the weaknesses of the other. Once there are a number of different possible solutions one can make a rational choice about which is best.

Often the initial idea is merely the pointer towards another, much more valuable, idea.

For instance, it might have led towards an idea manufactured by the German company, Miele: the Cat and Dog TT 5000 vacuum cleaner. This is a vacuum cleaner for pet owners that's designed to be particularly good at picking up pet fur from carpets. It even includes an activated carbon filter to deal with nasty smells. The appearance is less exciting than a combined toy dog and vacuum cleaner, but it meets a much broader unmet need and hence makes a lot more money.

Finding and specifying the area in which you want to work can often be half the work.

As the philosopher John Dewey (1859–1952) said, "A problem well stated is half solved." This is very true. In 1995, when Ann Pettifor started working in a draughty plastic shed on the roof of the Christian Aid building in London, trying to do something about third-world debt, nobody believed the public would take an interest in sovereign debts or engage in arcane arguments about the international financial system. She says that it took her two of the five years of the campaign to find the right way to explain what the campaign wanted to achieve, so that it would cut to the essence of the problem but also engage the public. Her phrase for this process is "cutting the diamond". By 1997 her team had articulated the key "ask", which became summarized as "drop the debt". The campaign name of Jubilee 2000 emerged when Martin Dent – an academic from Keele – had the idea of linking the new millennium and the campaign for the cancellation of unpayable third-world debt with the biblical principle of Jubilee, the Sabbath of Sabbaths at which debts were forgiven.[48]

Although (or perhaps because) they spent nearly half the duration of the campaign defining the "ask", ultimately the campaign engaged tens of millions of campaigners around the world, and it has resulted in $22 billion in debt relief for highly indebted poor countries.

People often fail to realize how important questions and problems are to creativity. They say, "That's not creativity, it's just problem solving."

This is unfortunate because if you insist that problem solving isn't true creativity, you are just reinforcing the idea that creativity is something rare and special that you don't have. This in turn damages your creative self-confidence.

However, the reality is that great engineers, artists and communicators all very often start the creative process by identifying or creating a "problem" that interests them and then nagging away at it until they have solved it.

For example, Maurice Cockrill started work on his "bridge" series of abstract paintings because he got interested in the problem of "how to represent the essence of water flowing under a bridge".[49]

He tells me that he quite explicitly formulated this as a problem and a question to focus his creative energies and then "held the space" into which his ideas flowed. Rather than starting immediately on the pictures in the series, he started by painting lots of little studies to explore his ideas, only later starting work on the final pictures.

Use ambiguity

A level of ambiguity can be really helpful when defining the objective. This is something that eastern cultures often feel much more comfortable with than western ones, and they can often use it very effectively. For example, in 1978, Honda top management decided that the Honda Civic and Accord models were becoming too familiar and they needed to do something new.[50] They called together a team of young engineers and designers (average age 27) and asked them to develop "a car that is inexpensive but not cheap. A product concept that is fundamentally different from anything we've done before."

This may sound vague, but it gave a clear sense of direction and boundaries while the ambiguity gave creative freedom to the team. The team was clear that they were being asked to do something radical, but that it should still be a car. Top management was not asking them for aerospace ideas, but neither did they want minor modifications of existing models. This meant that the team rapidly rejected one early idea of just making a smaller, cheaper version of the Honda Civic.

At the time, cars in Japan were long, low sedans, following the styling of cars designed for the wide open roads of America, but very inappropriate for Japan's crowded roads and cities. The team came up with the idea of a fundamental guiding principle that they called "man maximum, machine minimum". This then developed into a car concept called "Tall Boy". They reasoned that this would be lighter and cheaper, but more comfortable and solid than traditional cars. It would also take up less space on the road.

This concept was launched as the Honda City: the world's first tall short car. At only 3.4m long, it was 40% shorter than the 1976 Ford Thunderbird.

The idea of the tall short car spread steadily round the world, so they are now ubiquitous in urban areas. Mercedes/DaimlerChrysler's Smart car is one of the most extreme examples, at only 2.5m long. This has been on sale in Europe since 1998, and was launched in the USA in 2008.

Ambiguity is also at the heart of one of the most important ideas of all time: Christianity.

Between AD 325 and AD 451, the early Church held four great "ecumenical councils" to clarify (and, for some, define) what the Christian scriptures taught and what the early Church believed about God, Jesus and Mary.

The fourth of these, the Council of Chalcedon (in modern Turkey), focused on Christ's human and divine nature. As the Right Reverend Tom Butler, Bishop of Southwark, says:

> *The Church attempted to define the nature of Jesus Christ, both God and Man, both Man and God. The council wasn't so much trying to explain the paradox as to define it, spell it out, to protect it from denial. It was those who were trying to avoid the paradox by making everything clear in one direction or another who came to grief and were denounced as heretics.*[51]

Important ideas always involve a level of ambiguity and uncertainty, so by recognizing and giving space to this you can help your ideas develop and spread. As Vroomfondel, the representative of the Amalgamated Union of Philosophers, Sages, Luminaries and Other Thinking Persons, said in the cult British comedy series *Hitchhiker's Guide to the Galaxy*, "We demand rigorously defined areas of doubt and uncertainty."[52]

This is quite a neat encapsulation of the requirement for ambiguity in developing great ideas!

Focus on the question, not the idea

It is very powerful to start by focusing on the question, not the idea.

I've run, or worked in, innovation teams for over 20 years. During this time we probably worked on over 300 inventions. Our experience showed that the first idea was often a good pointer to an underlying need, but was very seldom the best idea for a solution, even though it would often feel brilliant at the time.

We found that the best process for inventing things was to start with a seed idea (if we had one), but use this to help us define the unmet need and constraints. We would then use the question "How can we … ?" to stimulate us to generate a variety of different solutions. One of these might well be the original idea, but we found that aiming to produce five to ten different concepts over a month or two seemed to be about optimum. We would then get some people who had appropriate expertise, but hadn't been involved in developing the ideas, to help us review them in order to choose the top two or three. We'd develop these some more, and then choose the best idea.

Only then did we start developing a prototype of the idea.

Sometimes we gave in to the temptation to skip this stage and just developed our first idea because it seemed so brilliant (at the time), but over the years it became clear: our chances of success were around ten times higher if we resisted the temptation and started with a question about an unmet need, rather than an idea.

People sometimes ask how we had time to develop ten solutions rather than one. The trick is not to take the initial concepts too far; we would just aim to get a clear vision of how each idea would work and to think about its strengths and weaknesses. Often a hand-drawn sketch would be sufficient.

The sketch on the next page shows one of over 20 different concepts for the Tool-free blade-changing mechanism that I developed for Bosch jigsaws. The photograph is of the final product.

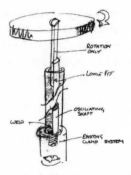

Concept 19: This idea is a built-in "screwdriver" for tightening up the clamp screw that holds the saw blade in position. The design means that the handle of the "screwdriver" stays still, even while the saw blade is being moved up and down by the power tool's motor
© Anne Miller

Final product: The lighter coloured button in the centre of the black knob is pressed down to turn it into the handle of a built-in screwdriver. The mechanism inside is very similar to the concept sketch, but it includes an additional mechanism to make a definitive "click" when the blade is securely clamped   © Tom Bragg

Many innovative development teams use similar processes. The principle of looking for multiple solutions to a problem is considered normal in Japan. It is perhaps unfortunate that in the West we are sometimes influenced by a feeling that there has to be "one right answer", and so we focus exclusively on one idea much too soon.

The time invested in generating these alternatives at the beginning pays off because it reduces the risk of getting halfway through a development and realizing that you are developing the wrong idea. It also helps our creativity by encouraging us to explore in an area of interest, because this "problem finding" process is an important part of the creative process. The psychologists Jacob Getzels and Mihaly Csikszentmihalyi have found that artists produced work of higher-rated quality when they did not start with a definite plan in mind, but concerned themselves instead with exploring and discovering emerging structures and forms.[53]

Secondly, by having alternatives to consider, we avoid the problems of "confirmation bias" and can make better quality decisions on the merits of our ideas and redirect them more effectively. Confirmation bias is a well recognized psychological tendency to seek out information to confirm an idea or hypothesis, rather than to try to find evidence to reject it.

One classic demonstration of this is the 2-4-6 task, developed by the creative psychologist Peter Wason in 1960. To try this out on your friends choose a sequence of three numbers, for example 2-4-6, and ask them to find out the rule you used to generate it. They do this by proposing sequences and you then tell them if their sequence is permitted by your rule or not.

Their guesses might go as follows:

		Does it fit your rule?	Guessed rule	Guesser's confidence
Starting point	2-4-6			
Guess 1	4-6-8	yes	Increase by 2s	50%
Guess 2	5-7-9	yes	Increase by 2s	70%
Guess 3	20-22-24	yes	Increase by 2s	100%

When they feel they are 100% confident, they tell you what they think your rule was and you tell them whether they are right or not. If, as in Wason's experiments, you chose a simple rule, such as "increasing numbers", they will probably be surprised to find that they have got it wrong.

Although there are lots of possible rules you could have used, for example "increasing numbers" or "adds up to 12" or "any even number", people will normally feel they are confident after remarkably few guesses.

Confirmation bias means that they are much more likely to test you on sequences that they think fit their guessed rule, rather than to test their hypothesis by trying out sequences that they think *won't* fit. If you had a rule like "increasing numbers", which is not encompassed by the narrower, more obvious rule "increasing by 2s", this bias makes it very difficult for them to uncover the right answer.

On the other hand, if the guesser had thought the rule was "increase by 2s" but decided to test it by trying something they thought would disobey the rule, such as 4-6-7, they would have been surprised to get the answer that it *did* obey the rule. This would then set them off on the track of exploring why. They might then have made a sequence of guesses like these, and discovered the correct answer:

		Does it fit your rule?	Guessed rule	Guesser's confidence
Starting point	2-4-6			
Guess 1	4-6-8	yes	Increase by 2s	50%
Guess 2	4-6-7	yes	Increase by 2s	0%
Guess 3	5-6-7	yes	Increasing	50%
Guess 4	6-3-13	no	Increasing	70%
Guess 5	6-4-2	no	Increasing	90%
Guess 6	3-9-22	yes	Increasing	100%

They would then have a chance of uncovering a simple broader rule such as "increasing numbers".

We suffer from a similar bias when trying to assess our ideas. We can be good at asking the questions that assume that our ideas are OK but just need a little refinement, but tend to be very poor at asking the questions that will show us that we need a complete change of direction.

However, just as we saw when discussing the combined toy dog and vacuum cleaner, if we are exploring and assessing several different ideas simultaneously, it reduces the danger of confirmation bias because the questions we ask while trying to refine one idea can help redirect another.

Realism about constraints

Once we have a clear objective and focus for our work we need to define the constraints.

Constraints often feel very frustrating. People insist on telling you that your great idea won't work, or as happened with Wegener's theory of continental drift, they persist in pointing out the "numerous flaws". When this happens, it's very tempting either to ignore them, or to get so discouraged that you stop work.

However, even if ultimately you will succeed in proving your critics wrong, it's better to question them and listen hard to what they say. Face up to the mental conflict this produces between your vision and the inconvenient truths in the way, and divert it into creative energy.

Facing up to reality and giving our ideas meaningful constraints increase the chances that they will be practical and workable. Constraints also help stimulate our creativity.

The battle to overcome constraints is a fundamental source of creativity. The Hungarian polymath Arthur Koestler suggested in 1964 that creativity arises out of unconscious conflict, as contrary ideas or patterns are brought together.[54] The psychoanalysts take it a stage further, so Freud even analyzed the work of Leonardo da Vinci, examining its symbolic content for evidence of repressed sexual conflict.[55]

The cognitive psychologists Ronald Finke, Thomas Ward and Steven Smith at the Texas A&M University carried out a very interesting series of experiments investigating the conditions that help creativity.[56] One of these explored the effect of constraints on people's ability to invent.

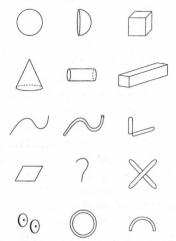

Subjects were given two minutes to mentally arrange three object parts to create a practical device in an assigned category, for example Furniture, Weapons, Transportation, etc.

The object parts all came from a predefined list. In some of the experiments the subjects were allowed to choose which three object parts they would like to use, in other cases they were assigned three object parts at random. After their two minutes they sketched their results and independent judges rated the results to decide on the number of practical and creative solutions.

Object parts used in creative invention experiments

These experiments showed that having tighter constraints helped creativity. Even though they only had two minutes, remarkably 49% of people came up with a practical solution, and 14% a creative one. They were nearly three times more likely to produce a creative solution if they were assigned the object parts than

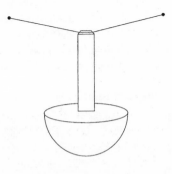

Hip exerciser invented by student
Both from Ronald A. Finke, *Creative Imagery: Discoveries and Inventions in Visualisation*[57]

if they were allowed to choose which ones they wanted to use. They were only very slightly less likely to come up with a practical solution.

There are some limits on how tight constraints can be, however. If people were assigned object parts and then told to invent not just something in a particular category, like a piece of furniture, but a more specific device within that category, such as a chair or a table, it became much harder for them to come up with either a practical or a creative solution. This is because the features of a something like a chair or table are more specialized, and hence it might not be possible to include these features from a random selection of object parts.

Structured imagination

Listening to our critics and accepting unwelcome constraints will help us develop better ideas, and ideas that will be more likely to be accepted (even if they are bad). However, we must choose our constraints well – conventional constraints lead to conventional results, just as our past experience tends to structure our thinking and limit our imagination.

The engineers developing the first railway carriages in the 1830s had previously designed stagecoaches. Their past experience meant they did not have to start from scratch, but it also structured their imagination, so the first trains were constructed of separate carriages, very like stagecoaches with external brakes and running boards but with no interconnecting passage. The conductors rode on top at the front, and had to clamber around the outside. This was a dangerous activity, so injuries and fatalities were common. Later designs incorporated an internal aisle, though this idea met with some resistance, because people were afraid it would become a mobile spittoon. Although American trains were redesigned almost immediately to allow people to move more easily between carriages, in the UK the carriages remained separate for much longer, and it was not until about 1994 that the last carriages without interconnecting gangways were finally phased out on personal safety grounds.[58]

False constraints

It is very common to assume the existence of false constraints.

As the inventor of the manufacturing machine for the Femidom,[59] the surprisingly large female condom, I used to get approached regularly by amateur condom inventors. In 2003 I was approached by a Portuguese inventor of an AIDS-proof condom. He was very upset, because he felt his ideas could make a difference, but they were being ignored.

In my opinion, he was getting rejected for two reasons.

Firstly, his condom had sharp corners. This might have been something one could overcome by making the prototypes in a different way, but it didn't give a very reassuring first impression.

Secondly, it was about as stiff and unappealing as a plastic take-away container. This was because he had put a lot of effort into finding materials that he thought would be proof against the AIDS virus and guaranteed burst-proof, and so hadn't allowed himself to use thinner and more flexible materials.

He'd been inspired to invent it because of claims by the Vatican that the HIV virus was small enough to pass through the latex of ordinary condoms. Unfortunately, though perhaps understandably, he hadn't questioned these claims and so was unaware of the scientific consensus stating unambiguously that the existing materials are fine, and the virus cannot pass through.[60] Scientific consensus doesn't have to be right, but it's noticeable that the Vatican quietly dropped the claim after the initial flurry of press coverage.

He was so attached to this constraint that he found it very hard to understand why others were uninterested in his idea. I suspect that he was doomed to disappointment because the people who would most readily accept the Vatican's claims would be the ones least likely to be interested in contraceptives. The people most likely to be receptive to ideas for improved condoms would, like me, be most sceptical about the constraints he'd imposed on himself.

It is now apparent that behind the scenes in the Vatican a theological debate was taking place, driven by the first-hand experience of the impact of HIV/AIDS by Roman Catholic missionaries and pastors in the developing world. In 1988 Pope John Paul II's own theologian, Cardinal Georges Cottier, signalled the doubts within the papal household and argued that the Roman Catholic "theology of life" could be used to justify lifting of the ban on using contraception. Later, Cardinal Barragán, Pope Benedict XVI's "health minister", noted a passage from a 1981 document issued by the late Pope John Paul II. This said that "every conjugal act must be open to life".

Until recently, this had been interpreted as an injunction against contraception. But it could also be used to support an argument in favour of the preservation of life by the use of barrier methods.

In 2006 the Italian newspaper *La Repubblica* broke the news of the policy review and reported that the Vatican would "go from prohibition to the definition of exceptional cases in which it would be possible for the faithful to use prophylactics to avert fatal risks".

If correct, this thoughtful and creative policy review within the Vatican will do a lot more to help Catholics reconcile their faith with the need to do something about HIV/AIDS than would the inventor's idea for a rather unpleasant AIDS-proof condom.

The inventor was reluctant to question the Vatican's pronouncements, but we can all jump to false conclusions that make life harder for ourselves. We are most likely to impose a false constraint on ourselves where we are under stress, or feel anxious about questioning it. Sometimes this is because of the authority of the person we perceive as setting the constraint. In other cases, our expectations mislead us, so, for example, in one organization I worked with, one of the managers interpreted the board's vague expression of a preference as an edict, because she had been expecting them to make problems. It was only later when I encouraged her to question what they really meant that she realized that they actually rather liked her idea.

In other cases we feel nervous about talking to the people we think will benefit from our idea, and so just assume we know what they want. In another AIDS-related example, I was once approached by an inventor with an idea to help the gay community avoid infecting each other in clubs. It sounded a bit naive to me, but I was even more sceptical when he admitted that he hadn't had the courage to talk about it to anyone who was gay.

As we saw with "confirmation bias", we can improve the quality of our ideas by training ourselves to explore our constraints and find the true boundaries of what is and is not acceptable.

It can be very productive to try temporarily switching the emphasis between the different constraints. For example, if you are trying to provide an improved service as cheaply as possible, spend a while generating some ideas that make it as friendly as possible, as efficient as possible or as high tech as possible.

One enjoyable and effective creativity technique is to imagine, "Wouldn't it be wonderful if… ?", and temporarily allow something completely impossible to happen. For example, a few years ago a major oil company was struggling to resolve a shortage of staff on an oil platform in the North Sea between the UK and Norway.[61] To loosen up their thinking they played with imagining what they could do if they'd drained the North Sea! Someone suggested bringing in caravans and parking them around the platform to accommodate extra staff. They then realized that even if the sea was back in place, they could bring in Portakabins, stack them up on the platform, bring in extra staff and pay them a bonus for being temporarily overcrowded.

It's also productive to ask yourself how the constraints on you are different from those on your competitors. It's very common for people to say,

"Product X is ridiculously expensive, but my idea is going to be cheaper." The key question I always ask is "Why?"

If the answer is that you have the financial backing to make and sell it in much larger quantities (which tends to allow things to be cheaper), then it's quite convincing. You might also be less constrained by the baggage of previous ways of doing it, or aiming to produce something for a slightly different market that will be quite happy with a less sophisticated product.

However, many people have no clear rationale to explain why they are likely to be more successful than their predecessors, and this makes me very sceptical about their chances. It is by identifying these areas where your constraints give you a unique advantage that you can decide how best to focus your creativity to give your ideas the best chance. As we will see in Chapter 7, you will also find these arguments really helpful when later you need to convince some of the Careful Conservator types about the merits of your idea.

Finally, one of the most powerful ways to explore and test your constraints is to get constructive criticism of your ideas. If you are working in a big corporation, you may feel that you get too much criticism and have far too many stupid constraints imposed upon you already. If you are independent and free, however, lack of constructive criticism can be a big problem. Part of the problem is that it's so nice to avoid the pain of having your ideas criticized that it's very easy to keep on postponing the moment when you expose them to criticism and possible new constraints.

Your very independence and isolation may mean that you're pursuing an idea that's rubbish: totally unrelated to a real need, or deeply impractical. Even if you've been spot on in targeting your efforts on a real opportunity, without external criticism it's very easy to carry on elaborating your ideas way past the point where they're useful. You're then likely to become very frustrated by the world's refusal to listen when you do finally tell people about it.

An experienced and creative engineer told me of how he'd invented a new way of feeding ink in an office printer. It was very simple, with only a few components. He then continued developing and elaborating the idea and after six months had a concept for a completely new printer, incorporating his clever ink system. However, when he started trying to excite printer manufacturers about it he found that they loved his ink feeding idea, but hated the surrounding printer; he'd used his freedom to take his idea too far, past the point that inventors call "maximum magic".[62]

He realized to his disappointment that he should have stopped working on his idea six months earlier, and saved himself a lot of time and effort.

Inventors are often worried that someone will steal their idea if they reveal it. Clearly, if you genuinely have something valuable, you will need to take professional advice (e.g. from a patent agent) about how to protect your idea before disclosing it. However, I find that in the very early stages theft is much less of a problem than people think: just as it is hard to get people to adopt your idea, you will also find that you can discuss it surprisingly freely without people taking any notice. In the early stages, the best way to allow discussions in safety is often just to get people to sign a "non-disclosure agreement" (companies will often have a standard one they want to use). Alternatively, if this seems too formal because you just want feedback on some aspect of the idea, give people a few misleading hints about what it's about and when they jump to the wrong conclusion, reinforce it by saying vaguely, "Yes, something like that..."

This will send them off on the wrong track, and your secret will be safe. This works remarkably well for gathering the information and feedback you need to turn a seed idea into a great idea.

The most successful creative people generate lots of ideas but also tend to be extremely good at filtering out their own bad ones. The psychologist Mihaly Csikszentmihalyi quotes the inventor Jacob Ranibow saying, "You cannot think only of good ideas... If you're good, you must be able to throw out the junk immediately without even saying it."[63]

Only when you can combine the power of your vision with the grounding of reality will your ideas be ready to face their next challenge: persuading the world to listen.

Before you move on, take a few minutes to reflect back over the ideas of the last three chapters, and turn to the back of the book to note down the three ideas from each chapter that you most want to remember for the future. If you skipped over the personality test, this is a good time to try it.

PART

2

Dealing with resistance

Blind

"What idea?"

The world will beat a path to your door, they say, but often it seems as if people wilfully ignore completely obvious ideas in the face of overwhelming evidence.

The inventor seems blind to the flaws in her invention, even though it's obviously barmy.

The oilman refuses to believe that burning fossil fuels causes climate change, citing increasingly bizarre nonentities in preference to the world's top scientists.

The old-fashioned chauvinist thinks that women are inferior and refuses to be convinced by examples to disprove it.

We wonder: Are they stupid? Are they just pretending? How could they be so blind?

Talking about blindness is not just a metaphor. As we'll see in this chapter, one of the most fundamental problems with new ideas is that our brains are designed so that our perceptions of the world around us are filtered and forced to fit in with what we expect. If they don't fit (and radical new ideas tend not to fit) the perceptions will be ignored.

This means that our first task in persuading someone to adopt a new idea is to understand this blindness, and how to break through it.

Blindness to new ideas

This blindness is very common in the world of innovation and ideas.

In the late 1980s Coca-Cola marketing executives in Chicago had spent three years assessing the market for flavoured water. Some years later, one former manager told me that suddenly, to their horror, they found that a small Canadian company had appeared, producing just what they had been considering. She said, "They came from nowhere. They were everywhere."

The Coca-Cola executives were really puzzled. How had this competitor moved so fast?

The answer wasn't really that the Clearly Canadian Beverage Corporation had moved so fast (although little companies do move faster than large bureaucracies), but that they had been quietly building up sales outlets and distribution chains all around Coca-Cola's headquarters, unnoticed. The executives at Coca-Cola were so busy paying attention to their internal analysis of the market that they were blind to this, until Clearly Canadian's unusual pear-shaped, blue-glass bottles were everywhere, standing out amongst the sea of cans and plastic in the stores all around them.

In the world of fizzy drink marketing, this was big stuff.

Clearly Canadian proudly, and perhaps rightly, claim, "Clearly Canadian's launch of its brand of sparkling flavoured water, with its natural flavours and distinctive packaging, helped usher in a whole new era in drinks – blazing the trail for what is now known as the Alternative Beverage category, a category currently estimated at $14 billion within North America alone."[64]

Blindness is very common, even with things that one would think should be rather more significant and noticeable than a new brand of fizzy drink.

Dramatic "disruptive" innovations are very seldom produced by the dominant players in the market. The history of technology shows repeated cycles in which the unnoticed underdog takes over the dominant position.

The successive waves of invention that led from the first commercial typewriter to the PC illustrate this well.[65]

In 1874 Remington launched the first commercial typewriter. It was cumbersome and noisy, and you couldn't see what you were typing, but over the next decade it steadily improved and became ubiquitous in offices. Remington were still the clear top dog in typewriters in 1890, but by 1899 were seriously under threat.

Inventor Franz Wagner had designed a machine on which you could see the type, but it was John Underwood and his father, who were in the ribbon and carbon paper business, who spotted the potential for it, bought the design and put it into production.

Underwood's machines had the look and feel of today's manual typewriter and dominated the market for half a century, but during the disruption of the Second World War and the subsequent economic boom they failed to address the rise of the electric typewriter.

Electric typewriters were initially unpopular, but by 1967 30% of all typewriter sales went to IBM's electric typewriter, and what was now Olivetti-Underwood had only 10%. By the mid 1970s, IBM was on the way down again, and was only one amongst about 55 different companies that were offering the next new invention: stand-alone word processors with a screen, printer and text-processing software. Although IBM was big in mainframe computers, it also missed the start of the next wave of invention, the personal computer.

The first true PC was produced by Altair, a manufacturer of electronic kits, but by 1977 Altair's PC had been joined by at least thirty others, of which the most successful was the Apple II, the predecessor of the successful Apple Mac today.

IBM only regained its position with the launch of the first IBM PC in 1981. This was no technological breakthrough, and in many respects was worse than the Apple, but it quickly took 30% of the business market. The only real innovation was IBM's open architecture, which allowed other companies to develop and supply "IBM compatible" software, peripherals and machines, so it rapidly developed into a global standard for PCs. This was very important for the industry, but over the years IBM steadily lost their dominant position as other manufacturers produced PC clones and the PC became a commodity.

IBM were focused on the hardware of the machines, and hadn't realized how important software was to become, so in 1980 when they contracted Microsoft to develop the operating system for the PC, they allowed Bill Gates to retain the rights to license it to other companies. This was a very smart piece of negotiation by Bill Gates, because, as every PC needed an operating system, this became worth a fortune.

Twenty years later, the real winners weren't the manufacturers of the hardware of the PC itself, but the software manufacturers: by 2005 Microsoft was valued at $240 billion, 200 times more than IBM's entire PC division.

The story doesn't end there, because the next wave seems to be about the content and how it's communicated, rather than the computing. By 2006 the upstart search engine Google was worth more than the whole of IBM and over half of Microsoft.

Big corporations throw resources at "scenario planning", trying to predict the future. Nevertheless, as the history of disruptive innovation shows, they very often miss what is growing under their noses and get it spectacularly wrong. In 1945, Thomas Watson, chairman of IBM, estimated that the world market for computers was about five. By 2008 it was estimated that there were over one billion PCs in use in the world, one for every seven people on the planet.

Science-fiction writers are much more imaginative than corporations and their imagination is not constrained by a corporation's investment in the status quo. However, they still fall into the same trap of excessively extrapolating the high visibility trends and ignoring the potential for rapid and disruptive change.

In the 1960s it was quite common for science fiction writers to assume that every home would be heated by its own nuclear reactor and that we would be travelling to the stars in spaceships designed by engineers using slide rules. A mere 15 years later, electronic calculators took over from slide rules, consigning the few that remain to the backs of engineers' dusty cupboards. In 1979, the near nuclear disaster of the reactor at Three Mile Island in Pennsylvania intensified public fear of nuclear power to the extent that no new reactors have been built in the USA since. It also became clear that the insurance and decommissioning costs made nuclear power commercially unviable without state subsidy. Today, the rise in international terrorism and fears of proliferation mean that the idea of having a nuclear reactor in your kitchen seems laughable, although concern about climate change and energy security is giving nuclear power a second chance.

Science-fiction authors and corporations both tend to be wrong in their forecasts because we extrapolate current trends excessively, and ignore the potential for rapid and disruptive change. As we'll see later, our world view and past experience are so important in determining what we can perceive that we ignore things that don't fit, or force fit them into pigeonholes that do fit.

This blindness is a fundamentally important part of why radical ideas start by being ignored. It is also important in our senses, such as vision and hearing, in how people develop rigid stereotyped views, and how some ideas come to be seen as common sense while others are ignored. This effect is often referred to as "inattentional blindness".

Inattentional blindness

Inattentional blindness is particularly serious if one is driving at the time and is one of the reasons why a very common statement after a car accident is "He came from nowhere – I didn't see him." This is such a common phenomenon that in the transport field it's called "looked but failed to see". Research by the UK's Transport and Road Research Laboratory in the 1970s showed that this was responsible for 10% of drivers' errors, ranking third in order of importance after "lack of care" and "driving too fast".[66] It was recorded as a contributory factor in 21% of accidents at road junctions. In about half of the cases, this was due to a genuine cognitive limitation in the way we perceive confusing or unexpected things, and not to incorrect judgement, simple absentmindedness, or vehicles being hidden by something else.

As the psychologist Professor Kåre Rumar points out, "looked but failed to see" is bad news for the most vulnerable road users. He said:

Road users look in the appropriate direction at the appropriate moment, but they usually look for cars. This is very natural behaviour since cars are often the largest, heaviest, fastest and consequently the most dangerous objects visible. Unfortunately, after doing this and seeing no car within a critical distance, they complete the action and hit or are hit by a cyclist, a motorcyclist or even by a pedestrian.[67]

Objects don't have to be subtle for us to ignore them. Amazingly, when a motorway lane is closed off, people will sometimes drive straight into the lane-closure trailer, flashing lights and all. This means that the designers of lane closure trailers have to put a lot of effort into designing them to cope with the impact and still protect the workforce and the car driver.

The cognitive psychologists Daniel Simons and Christopher Chabris, while at Harvard University, did some fascinating work on "inattentional blindness",[68] the cognitive mechanism behind "looked but failed to see". A description of their work and the film clips they used in their experiments is available online or as a DVD so you can try them out on your friends.[69]

One of their most famous experiments shows a group of six students bouncing two basket balls between them in a corridor of the university building. The task is to watch the video, and count the number of passes made by the players in white. This is quite hard, because the students keep moving around and there are two balls in play, but people usually get roughly the right answer.

The experimenter (which is you if you are trying this on your friends) then asks the experimental subjects if anything unusual happened during the video clip.

About half of them won't have noticed that a gorilla walked across the screen during the ball game, stopped, beat its chest for a few seconds and then walked away. Many will refuse to believe it even when you tell them and a few won't even notice this on the second attempt, when they know what to expect. This is relatively rare, but I find that it seems to be the most diligent business people who can get so distracted by the counting task that they forget to look for the gorilla; they then get very embarrassed!

Simons and Chabris suggest that this is because the more an unexpected event shares the basic visual features that we are looking for, the more likely we are to see it. For example, if people are asked to pay attention to the black team rather than the white one, they are about twice as likely to notice the black gorilla. As one might expect, big, visually distinctive things are slightly easier to see than smaller ones, so when they ran similar experiments in which a woman with an umbrella walked though the group, she was noticed about 50% more frequently than the gorilla. This was probably because she was taller than the other players in the ball game, and the umbrella made her more visually distinctive. Nevertheless, about 30% of people will miss a bright red shape moving through a display that's otherwise all black and white.

It seems to make very little difference whether or not the event is inherently interesting to us; if it's unexpected in the context of the task that we are focusing on at that moment, we're likely to ignore it. Although it wasn't part of these experiments, the effect is so strong that it has been suggested that even if one replaced the gorilla with a scantily dressed young woman, many heterosexual men would probably still fail to notice that anything unexpected had happened!

The key message from this work is that if it's not expected in the "task context", or at least, not similar to the things we expect to see, we simply don't notice it. It's like completely meaningless background noise.

The cognitive psychologist Donald Broadbent became interested in how our attention works before the phenomenon of inattentional blindness had been systematically studied or named, but his work is still very relevant to explaining what's going on.[70] He suggested that there are two key processes at work: filtering and force-fitting.

Filtering

Basically, we filter everything out unless it's fundamentally distinctive and interesting or looks like something that we are paying attention to. This is a simple and fast process that uses very simple features such as shape, colour or sex to distinguish important things from irrelevant ones. This is great for letting us react quickly to a lot of complicated information without needing to pay the irrelevant things any active attention at all. The motorcyclist isn't the right shape for a car. The gorilla isn't white. We treat them like spam and ignore them.

We will also filter out things that don't fit with our mental model of the world. If the chauvinist is looking for candidates to promote to the board but believes that bosses need to be big men, a petite female applicant will rapidly be filtered out because she won't have the "features" he is looking for. Similarly, the job application from a young man who wants to work as a nurse may be unfairly filtered out by someone who believes that good nurses need to have "a woman's touch".

Filtering is vital, but its weakness is that it leads to errors if just one feature is misinterpreted or if the wrong features have been used for the filter. A collision is almost inevitable if a driver is only attending to one feature of a potential hazard, like the size or position of nearby vehicles, but is ignoring the speed of smaller and more distant vehicles.

Force-fitting or pigeonholing

The second process at work is pigeonholing. Broadbent points out that "there is a set of responses or pigeonholes ... into which any event in the environment will be forced if possible, or rejected if it fails to fit any of them."

Pigeonholing is used after filtering when we need to use a combination of features to decide whether something is relevant, such as whether an approaching but distant and slow-moving vehicle is safe.

This is slower, as it requires attention, and various features have to be processed in sequence and then combined into a sense of a coherent object. It is also prone to errors as features are combined and the results force-fitted into a pigeonhole.

This can produce bizarre results.

Consider the picture of Leonardo da Vinci's *Mona Lisa* on the next page.[71]

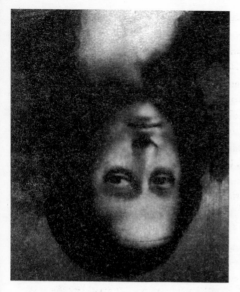

Is anything wrong?   Modifications © Anne Miller

Is anything wrong with it? When you have decided, turn the book upside down to see if you were right.

Most people will recognize the famous picture, even upside down, but will be surprised by how radically it changes when turned the right way up. This change in our perceptions is because an upside-down face is treated as an object by the brain, and processed as a whole. This makes us particularly vulnerable to force-fitting the elements into the familiar image. However, when it is turned the right way up it is processed as a face. Faces are very important to us, so the different elements are processed individually. This makes it immediately obvious that the face no longer has the enigmatic smile of the original.

Force-fitting can also happen between things that we attend to in quick succession.

This is because attention has been likened to the "glue" which binds things together into a coherent object, so long as they are seen in sufficiently rapid succession. This can sometimes produce misleading effects in which drivers unconsciously merge features from different vehicles. They can ignore a vehicle on a collision course because of the perception of safety they have formed from glancing at a slow-moving vehicle immediately beforehand, or merge the features of two vehicles seen at an accident into one.

This effect can "glue" together things that are perceived as much as half a second apart. Conversely, it also means that slow changes can be ignored. In another of Simons and Chabris's studies, an image changes over 12 seconds. Even though the changes are quite dramatic many people will fail to notice the change, and be very surprised by this when it is pointed out.

Force-fitting also happens with our hearing. If we walk into a crowded room, the voices may sound like an unintelligible hubbub, but if someone says our name, or something close to it, we hear it clearly amongst the confusion. Once again, we've automatically noticed something that is inherently distinctive and interesting, but have filtered out everything else.

Our expectations help us make sense of what we hear, but sometimes this can result in bizarre misunderstandings as we try to force-fit things into what we expect to hear. One excellent example of this is the claim that if you play Led Zeppelin's song "Stairway to Heaven" backwards, you can make out satanic messages. A nice demonstration of this is available online.[72] If you visit this site it is most interesting to start by hearing the song played backwards, but without the lyrics. It sounds vaguely like someone singing in a language you don't quite know. You can then play it a second time, with the satanic lyrics displayed. Suddenly, it becomes clear what the singer is saying; once you are reading the words you hear them all very clearly, although the accent is a little strange.

This is, of course, not a demonstration of satanic possession, but a demonstration of how our expectations influence our perceptions. Not only do we force-fit what we see into what we expect to see, we force-fit what we hear into what we expect to hear.

Unfortunately for our radically new idea, the same thing happens with ideas. If the people we tell our ideas to don't completely ignore them, force-fitting means that they say things like, "Oh that's just like my idea" or "We tried that years ago and it didn't work".

It may be true of course, but it may also be force-fitting at work.

If this happens it can be very effective to calmly probe them for the exact details of their idea, or what "exactly" they tried years ago.

Sometimes they will be silent, because they don't really have a reason, but are just trying to stall you for some other reason. However, very often you will find that either they can't really remember what they tried, or, if they can, you will discover that it differs significantly from your idea. Even if it is the same, the information about what exactly they tried and why it didn't work will very often be useful to help you build your idea.

By listening to them you are also helping get them on side with your idea. If they have the Careful Conservator or Innovative Trouble-Shooter personality, and like to trust their experience, by listening to their input you are helping make them feel that your idea is soundly grounded. If they are more of a Visionary Leader or Creative Maverick, by giving them the opportunity to contribute their ideas and insight you start to get them to feel involved.

In both cases, you are helping them integrate the idea into their own mental models for the way things are, or ought to be, which makes them more likely ultimately to accept it.

Mental models

The recipient's mental model is very important in determining whether ideas will be adopted as obvious, or whether the observations that might support them will be ignored or bizarrely misinterpreted. This is nicely illustrated by the very different dates in China and Europe for the discovery of sunspots.

Sunspots appear and disappear on the surface of the sun in a regular cycle. Usually they are too small to be seen with the naked eye, but when they are particularly large they can quite easily be seen at sunrise or sunset, when it's sometimes possible to look directly at the sun.

The Chinese have records of naked eye observations of sunspots back to 28 BC.[73] They had no problem seeing them, because the idea of sunspots coming and going on the surface of the sun fitted perfectly well with their worldview, which has the idea of change and cycles at its very heart. As the *Tao Te Ching* says in Chapter 36,

> *To shrink something*
> *You need to expand it first*
> *To weaken something*
> *You need to strengthen it first*
> *To abolish something*
> *You need to flourish it first*
> *To take something*
> *You need to give it first.*

However, in the European, Aristotelian mental model of the world the heavens were thought to be perfect and unchanging. It was unthinkable that black spots could come and go on the surface of the sun, so although dark spots had been observed on the sun at intervals, they tended to be ignored or interpreted as planets. A very large spot seen for no less than eight days in AD 807 was simply interpreted as the passage of Mercury in front of the sun. Even after the invention of the telescope in 1609, most observers of the heavens continued to interpret the spots as planets.

Three years later Galileo was probably the first European to see sunspots and correctly identify them as spots on the surface of the sun, more than 1,600 years after the Chinese.

As we'll see later in this chapter, our cultural differences can be very significant, affecting our perceptions and expectations in much more profound ways than we might expect because they have such an important influence on our mental models.

Mental models are useful and important because they help us make sense of the world around us.[74] They determine what we attend to, perceive, remember and understand, the goals we seek, how we organize our knowledge of the social world and what we think of as common sense.

Neuroscience suggests that mental models are based in the neural connections that are laid down in the brain to let us respond fast and appropriately in all sorts of situations: how to ride a bicycle, behave during a job interview, tell if someone of the opposite sex is interested in us, decide whether big two-legged feathered things like emus should be classified as birds or people, or how to decide whether event A caused event B. Some of these mental models we learn in childhood, others we learn much later in life.

If the environment we are in is consistent and our mental models prove useful and appropriate, these connections will continually be reinforced and hence become deeper and stronger. Steadily they become hardwired in.

This means that well-developed mental models become very strong and stable, and so can be very resistant to change.

Interconnections

Mental models are very interconnected. All sorts of social knowledge gets lumped together, so, for example, the mental model for a "party" might include the expectation that it would involve eating, drinking, dancing and having fun. They can also involve emotion, so we might associate fear with going to the dentist, or feel scepticism if we see a stereotypical politician making a speech. Everything tends to get switched on together, even if just one element of the model is triggered.

A particularly dramatic example of this is one of the survivors of the 7/7 terrorist bombing on the London Underground in 2005 who had been sitting only a few feet away from the suicide bomber when the bomb went off. He survived, but experienced flashbacks and an array of psychological symptoms. The strangest of these was that, if he found something funny, he would start laughing but this would immediately be replaced by an overwhelming rush of horror. Initially he couldn't understand why, but then he realized that at the moment of the explosion he'd reading a book by one of his favourite comic authors and had been laughing. The two emotions had become inappropriately linked in his mind.[75]

Important mental models are very similar to beliefs and are often linked together in a complex and reinforcing network. For example, if someone believes in God this will very seldom be isolated from their other beliefs, experiences, surroundings and personality. These will combine in complex ways to lead to quite different results in different people. One person's belief in God might link with an awareness of everyone's fundamental humanity and lead them to become an aid worker, devoting their life to helping the poor. Another's faith might link with a sense of an unjust oppression of their culture and religion, leading them to become a suicide bomber.

The cognitive-dissonance effect means that we find it very stressful to hold beliefs, attitudes and behaviours that are incompatible with each other. This means that if an idea attacks one aspect of a network of strongly embedded mental models and beliefs it will be ignored, or strongly resisted if it can't be ignored. Simply presenting evidence that shows that an element of an important mental model is wrong is as unlikely to work as signing up a hardened oilman to receive newsletters from Greenpeace or inviting a heart surgeon to a meeting of the Association of Crystal Healers.

As we will see in the next chapter, if we are trying to open people's eyes to our ideas, it's easiest and quickest if we can fit within their existing models, and learn to "speak their language". If that doesn't work we will have to trigger a more helpful alternative model, or else erode away the unhelpful model and rebuild a better one.

Reinforcement

Mental models can also tend to get unhealthily reinforced because, as we saw in Chapter 3, confirmation bias means that we have a tendency to seek out information that will confirm our point of view. The rise of the internet has made it increasingly easy for people to immerse themselves in a world of mutually reinforcing information, whether it's bizarre conspiracy theories, faith in obscure dietary supplements or fundamentalist religious beliefs.

This tendency to seek out information to reinforce our mental models can have disastrous consequences.

In 2006, the Iraq Study Group's report to the US administration on the deteriorating situation in Iraq commented that "Good policy is difficult to make when information is systematically collected in a way that minimizes its discrepancy with policy goals."[76]

As an example, the report detailed the way information was gathered on the violence.

> In addition, there is significant underreporting of the violence in Iraq. The standard for recording attacks acts as a filter to keep events out of reports and databases. A murder of an Iraqi is not necessarily counted as an attack.

If we cannot determine the source of a sectarian attack, that assault does not make it into the database. A roadside bomb or a rocket or mortar attack that doesn't hurt US personnel doesn't count. For example, on one day in July 2006 there were 93 attacks or significant acts of violence reported. Yet a careful review of the reports for that single day brought to light 1,100 acts of violence.

Not only do we tend to select our sources of information to fit with our mental models (even if we're not doing it deliberately for political reasons), but most of the time, most people will focus on the information that is consistent with their mental models.

For example, in one experiment, people were shown a video of a woman having dinner with her husband.[77] If they were told she was a librarian they would tend to remember things that fitted with their stereotypical view of librarians, perhaps that she wore glasses and drank wine. If they were told that she was a waitress, they were more likely to remember that she was drinking beer. These memories can then mislead us, reinforcing mental models and stereotypes that may not be justified.

Although most of the time people focus on things that are consistent with their mental models, in some situations people focus on things that are inconsistent. We see this in the irritating tendency of the boss to pick out and focus on the one area of our bright idea that's got a problem, while ignoring the 95% of it that's just fine.

Social psychologists suggest that this is because experts are much better than novices at noticing things that are inconsistent.

In one experiment in the 1980s, American students were grouped according to their political expertise.[78] They were then asked to read a description of Mauritius (a country none of them knew anything about) and answer questions on it. For half the students the description started by saying that Mauritius was a communist country. The other half were told that it was democratic. The description that followed was carefully balanced, referring both to things that the students would see as stereotypically communistic (political prisoners) and democratic (regular elections).

Students who were political novices tended to remember the information that fitted with their mental model for that type of political system, for example prisoners in a communistic state. The students with a more sophisticated understanding were more likely to notice the things that were less consistent with their mental model, for example that it was a democratically elected communistic state which held regular elections.

Cognitive psychologists suggest that this is because in experts' mental models the concepts are better organized and the detailed concepts are more strongly linked together. This means that while a novice is struggling to understand and remember the new information that's coming in, experts have enough spare working memory to pay attention to things that seem inconsistent. The difference is accentuated by the level of interest: if someone isn't that interested in an area, they will tend to skim over the information, but if they are more involved they will be prepared to put in more work to understand it.

This doesn't mean that the "experts" will like what they see, of course, but at least they notice it.

The implication of this is that, although most of the time our radical idea will just be ignored because it doesn't fit with people's mental models, if someone starts raising objections to our idea, we should take it as a good sign that we've broken through to the next stage in getting them to adopt it. We may then need to deal with them in a quite different way to the people who are still blind.

The combined effect of filtering, force-fitting, systematic selection and selective memories can give us very rigid, stable and strong mental models. This is important and useful in allowing us to respond quickly and appropriately in complex situations, but it is frustrating if you want to get a stereotype-busting idea across. The very rigidity and selectivity of the mental models means that, almost inevitably, they will be dysfunctional in times of change.

We are all vulnerable to the tendency to become fixated about our favourite ideas and ways of seeing the world, but I always rather like the "life-coaching" advice given by the Queen of Hearts to Alice in the children's classic, *Alice in Wonderland*, in which she said, "Why, sometimes I've believed as many as six impossible things before breakfast."

Playing with impossible ideas, reading impossible articles and talking with impossible people are great ways to keep your mental models flexible.

If you are serious about wanting to make a difference with your ideas this is worth doing. As anyone who assesses ideas professionally will tell you, one of the most common reasons that potentially interesting ideas fail to get exploited is the originator's rigidity. All too often people kill their chances of getting their ideas adopted by clinging too tightly to an unrealizable vision and refusing to make any compromises.

True creativity is the ability to keep focused on the essential essence of your vision, while being open, flexible and responsive about how to get there.

NIH and peer pressure

Developing rigid mental models and becoming blind to information that doesn't fit can be a problem for individuals, but it is even more of a danger for groups.

"Not Invented Here" syndrome, or NIH, is a syndrome well known to engineers. The phrase developed in the research and development community to describe the tendency of well-established groups to think that they have the monopoly on knowledge and hence reject any ideas that come from outside the group.

Initially NIH was just engineers' "folklore", but in 1982 the management professors Ralph Katz and Thomas Allen carried out a major research study to investigate it. They compared the performance of 50 different project groups within a large laboratory to see what happened to the vitality of the teams as the years went by.[79]

They found that for the first 18 months after its formation a team's performance tended to improve. This is what one would expect as people get to know and trust each other better, and to bond together. However, after as little as four years, performance was clearly on the decline, and after five years it was often no better than a newly formed team.

The team members were no less able than the members of the more newly formed teams, but were steadily tending to ignore and isolate themselves from their most important sources of information. If they were research engineers who most needed to access external information they tended to become inward-looking and ignore external ideas. If they were development engineers who really should have been exchanging ideas internally with the marketing group in order to develop a new product that people would actually want to buy, this was the area in which they ceased to communicate so effectively.

It was almost as if some demon was at work, selecting the most useful forms of communication for each team and then damaging it.

The researchers suggest that this is because individuals tend to organize themselves to reduce stress and uncertainty. This meant that they tended to ignore and become increasingly isolated from the sources of information that would provide the more critical kinds of evaluation, information and feedback. As time went on they became more and more comfortable with the security of their familiar environment and increasingly resistant to new ideas.

As one might expect, this self-imposed isolation meant that long-established teams also tended to develop their own language, jargon and mental models for what was going on.

The most effective way to reduce the development of NIH syndrome is to get new people to join the group at intervals. These newcomers provide a very important energizing and destabilizing effect. It's quite tough to be that newcomer, however, because another aspect of group behaviour means that it feels very uncomfortable not fitting in with the group consensus. You will have to conform and fit in with their mental models to some extent to be heard. But it is worth remembering that your very distinctiveness is of value to the team, even though they may not take kindly to being told so!

The psychologist Charlan Nemeth looked at the performance of juries, and found that having even one dissenter on the jury improved the quality of the decision, whether or not the dissenter was right.[80] This was because the challenge helped people start to question their assumptions, rather than blindly go along with their mental models.

Because our peers tend to use the same mental models, we tend to find them more believable, and hence we are more easily influenced by them. Although often this is frustrating if you are trying to get a new idea across, it is also possible to use it to your advantage.

The pharmaceutical company GlaxoSmithKline (GSK) was once assessing the performance of its various marketing activities and discovered to its surprise that the most cost effective activity was not its huge direct mail department, or any of the other traditional recipients of the marketing budget. The top performer was a small programme in which small groups of family doctors were brought together with a "neutral" facilitator to discuss how they treated a particular condition. This condition of course "just happened" to be one for which GSK had a treatment available. The facilitator didn't need to push the advantages of GSK's drug. The participants were aware that they were being hosted by GSK so the doctors that had had the best experiences with using GSK treatment for the condition tended to speak up most clearly. Those who were less happy tended to stay silent. This resulted in a very strong peer reinforcement effect and increased sales, all for the cost of a facilitator and a few biscuits.

This subtle approach was much more effective at getting GSK's idea across than any formal presentation would have been. This was because to the participants it felt like a discussion with colleagues, rather than ideas being pushed from "outside". This meant they relaxed the scepticism with which they would have listened to a normal commercial presentation, while the sense of supportive peer pressure acted to reinforce the views of the most voluble.

The same peer pressure technique can be used for almost anything.

In the 1970s Jacqueline Gold was working at her father's chain of rather seedy sex shops. "It wasn't a very nice atmosphere to work in," she said. "It was all men, it was the sex industry as we all perceive it to be."[81]

She didn't intend to stay in the job long, but by chance went to a Tupperware-style fashion party in an East London flat in 1981, where someone suggested she did the same for her father's company: give women the opportunity to group together in their homes to buy sexy lingerie and the latest sex toys. This was just the escape she was looking for, so she jumped at the idea. She tried running a few parties before pitching the idea to the rather reluctant, all-male board. As one might by now expect, because this idea didn't fit at all with their mental models about women and sex, they acted as if blind. One board member even said to her, "Well women aren't even interested in sex, so why would this idea work?"

She squeezed the idea through on her father's casting vote, and it became the immensely successful Ann Summers Party Plan, giving women an excuse to meet and talk about sex, while neatly getting around the legal restrictions limiting the presentation of sex toys in shops.

This built Ann Summers up from a chain of four shops in the 1970s to a multimillion-pound business with 7,500 party organizers, over 150 stores and sales of over £150 million.

Culture

If being part of a group can change our attitudes and mental models within four years, it's unsurprising that being part of a much larger group of people who have been together for hundreds, if not thousands, of years has a profound influence on our mental models.

These mental models form our very deep, underlying assumptions. For example, is the world fundamentally stable or in a continual state of flux? Is the best way to resolve a disagreement to use rhetoric and logic to decide who is right, or should you try to find the "middle way"? Should you try to develop children's individuality and self-esteem or teach them to fit in? East Asian and American cultures will tend to have very different answers to these questions.

Often these underlying assumptions are culturally determined, but although we seldom consciously notice them, they influence our attitudes and responses in critical ways. For example, polls in 2006 showed that 86% of people in Germany, France, Italy and the UK accept the idea that human actions are contributing to climate change,[82] but only 41% of Americans do.[83] Some of this difference may be due to the influence of a very professionally organized opposition within the USA, but cultural assumptions also play a role.

For example, the idea of human-induced climate change may be unwelcome, but it is not felt too unbelievable in crowded Europe, where human actions have fundamentally changed the landscape and environment for millennia. The variable but relatively clement weather in the UK means that the British are very aware of the weather, continually commenting on it to each other and changing their plans in response to it.

Getting across the idea of human-induced climate change may well be a much greater challenge to common underlying mental models in the USA where, only a few generations back, pioneers were still able to move west into virgin territory, leaving their environmental problems behind them. The more extreme climate there means that, in contrast to the UK, homes, offices and cars are air-conditioned and "climate control" is a daily reality.

These deep-seated mental models are particularly hard to change because we barely recognize that they exist. Nevertheless, dramatic changes in attitudes are possible. Whereas in 2003 only 17% of Americans thought climate change was a serious problem and that immediate action was required, three years later the proportion had nearly doubled.[84] There is still some way to go to reach the levels of concern in Japan, however, where in 2006 93% of the people surveyed said that they worried a "great deal or a fair amount" about climate change.[85] Japanese friends of mine living in the UK suggest that this very high level of concern may be because Japan is even more crowded than the UK, and is hit so frequently by natural disasters that it's impossible to feel complacent.

Our cultural background also influences our perception and our areas of blindness in surprising ways. As the University of Michigan psychologist Richard Nisbett points out in his fascinating book *The Geography of Thought*, people in eastern cultures tend to be more sensitive to relationships and the overall situation, while western cultures tend to focus more on the individual or the focal object.[86] For example, in one experiment students at Kyoto University and the University of Michigan were shown animated pictures of a fish tank. Each scene contained one or more "focal" fish that were larger, brighter and faster moving than anything else, together with a selection of plants, rocks, bubbles and slower moving fish, snails, frogs, and so on.

The students were shown the scene twice, then asked what they had seen. Although both groups referred roughly equally to the focal fish, the Japanese referred 60% more frequently to the background elements, and made twice as many references to the relationships involving the inert background objects. The difference in the focus of the students' attention was demonstrated clearly by the differences in the first sentence of the students' descriptions. While the first sentence from the Japanese was likely to refer to the environment – "It looks like a pond" – the American students were most likely to start by referring to the focal fish: "There was a big fish…"

This difference in our perceptions and attention starts at a very early age. Another experiment by the development psychologists Jessica Han, Michelle Leichtman and Qi Wang asked four- and six-year-old American and Chinese children to report on their day. While all the children talked about themselves more than about others, the proportion of self-references was more than three times higher for the American children than the Chinese children.

This difference in the emphasis given to the individual or to context probably helps explain why, historically, personality tests such as the MBTI instrument referred to in Chapter 2 have been so much more popular in the West than the East. Western cultures tend to assume that it's the individual and their personality that's important, while eastern ones tend to attach more importance to the group and the external environment that is influencing the individual. Both are, of course, very important, but our culture has a strong influence on our likely blind spots.

As part of this more holistic view of the world, easterners tend to see things as being interrelated to each other, so will want to consider more factors when making decisions about the world. This difference in emphasis is very evident when it comes to diagnosing technical faults. Western engineers are trained to look for "the right answer", so tend to start by looking for a single cause, and feel frustrated if addressing this doesn't fix the problem. They will come up with a statement like, "The machine failed because the component broke."

Japanese engineers expect to start by exploring root causes and identifying all the relevant contributory factors. For example, they'd say, "The machine failed because the component failed, and this was because there was a design weakness, the loads were unusually high, the inspection engineer was rushed and the assembly wasn't lubricated properly."

This approach may be slower initially, but in the long run it is highly effective.

The more holistic mindset typical amongst easterners helps reduce blindness to new information. Nisbett describes another experiment in which

Korean and American students were asked to decide which pieces of information were relevant to solving a detective mystery: the American students thought 55% of the information was irrelevant, while the Koreans rejected only 37%.

The eastern approach is not without problems, however. Whereas in the UK there is (or used to be) a perfectly acceptable stereotype of "the mad Englishman", in Japan the importance of maintaining group harmony means that they say, "The nail that sticks out is hammered down." This means that it's much easier to be a radical creative individual in the UK than Japan.

I suspect that this cultural difference helps explain why, historically, so many radical creative ideas were originated in the UK, from technological inventions like the LCD display or the MRI body-scanner, to innovative musical ideas, like the Beatles or punk rock. However, most of these new technical ideas were then exploited in Japan or the USA, because for some reason the UK has been very poor at the later stages of the process. This situation is unlikely to remain unchanged of course, because cultures evolve as they interact with each other, so it will be fascinating to see how both eastern and western cultures change with increasing globalization and the changing balance of economic power.

The difference in openness to new ideas can have serious consequences when a group is in trouble.

Culture is the source of our strength, because it is based on what worked well in the past. However, when times change it can easily become dysfunctional, and the later people leave it to change things, the more difficult it becomes. Firstly, this is because when people are under stress their attention narrows down, they become less perceptive, and less open to the new ideas that might save them. Secondly, as we will see in Chapter 6, when faced with an unwelcome idea, people very often become frozen, coming up with all sorts of excuses because they can't bring themselves to deal with it.

You see this in marriages facing divorce, companies facing receivership and even whole societies facing collapse. For example, at the end of the fourteenth century the last of the Norse settlers died in Greenland, while the Inuit prospered around them. As the award-winning scientist Jared Diamond points out in his book *Collapse*,[87] even though learning from the Inuit might have saved them from starvation, it seems that the Norsemen completely ignored the ideas and technology that were right in front of them.

The contrast between the attitudes of the Inuit and the Norsemen to new ideas is fascinating.

The Inuit seem to have been good at adopting ideas from others. They were the most recent of at least four successive waves of archeologically separate peoples, building on 4,000 years experience of living in the Arctic. In the eleventh or twelfth century, the Inuit overlapped with their predecessors, the Dorset people, for a few centuries, learning from them and then finally replacing them. This was probably because they had better technology – such as dogs and dogsleds, bows and arrows, kayaks and large sea-going boats of skin stretched over a framework, which allowed them to hunt whales at sea.

However, they weren't too proud to adopt technology and ideas from the Dorset people as well, and they took the ideas of a bone knife for cutting snow blocks, domed snow houses, soapstone technology and an improved design of harpoon head.

It also seems that they were interested in the Norsemen, and learned from them. There are at least 170 known Norse objects in Inuit sites, including a knife, shears and a firestarter, as well as pieces of metal that they would have valued for making their own tools. They must have met face to face with the Norsemen, because archaeologists have found nine Inuit carvings of Norse figures with characteristically Norse features such as the hairdo, clothes or a crucifix. They also learned to make barrel staves and screw-threaded arrowheads, something that would have been very hard to do without actually seeing it being done.

This made them very effective hunters, able to feed large communities in the harsh and variable arctic climate: one settlement, Sermermiut, on the western coast of Greenland, accumulated hundreds of dwellings.

In contrast, it seems that the Norsemen learned virtually nothing from the Inuit. There are very few references to the Inuit in Norse writings and very few Inuit artefacts at Norse sites, apart from some curiosities like an Inuit antler comb. They ignored technologies like the harpoon, spear thrower and kayak (which was much faster than any of their boats), and failed to learn from the Inuit how to hunt the ringed seal or the whale. Amazingly, all the evidence suggests that the Norsemen refused to eat fish, even though it was all around them and could have saved them from starvation.

They saw themselves as dairy farmers, Europeans and Christian, and clung stubbornly to their culture as the climate got slightly colder and times got harder. They lived primarily by pastoralism and hunting wild animals. They had large flocks of sheep and goats, but prized cows as status symbols, so devoted huge resources to growing and storing hay to feed them, even though the climate was thoroughly unsuitable. They built a large stone church, importing stained glass windows and communion wine from Europe, and followed the changing European fashions in clothes, jewellery and burial customs. Sadly, this focus on being more European than the Europeans meant that it was out of the question to imitate or intermarry with the Inuit.

Without their shared values it would have been impossible for them to have cooperated and survived for 450 years in such alien surroundings, but the stubbornness with which the Norsemen clung to their culture and refused to adopt new ideas was also their undoing.

Opening their eyes

AS WE SAW IN THE LAST CHAPTER, people ignore new ideas that don't fit with their important mental models, as if they were blind. This chapter discusses what one can do to open their eyes, so that they are at least aware of the existence of our idea, or the problem that it is trying to solve.

To do this we have three basic options. Firstly, we can try to fit within their existing mental models and "speak their language", but without being so boring that we're ignored. Secondly, if they are using unhelpful mental models to interpret the situation, we can try to trigger them to use more useful ones that may be present, but inactive. Finally, if all their existing mental models are too obstructive, we can embark on the longer and more difficult process of converting their existing mental models into more useful ones.

Speak their language

As the pioneering systems thinker Sir Geoffrey Vickers said, "New ideas must be expressed in the language of the old."

However, there is a balancing act to be performed. If you fit in too much, your ideas will seem so obvious and boring that they will be ignored. If you are too weird, your ideas will also be ignored. If you get it just right, you will at least be noticed, and your new ideas may well also start a steady process of evolution that will ultimately, in a small or major way, change how people view the world.

In the late 1980s, American AIDS activists did this very successfully. They faced the same problem Alfred Wegener had when trying to get across his idea of continental drift: influencing a tight community for whom they were alien outsiders. However the AIDS activists adopted a much more effective engagement strategy than Wegener and got their ideas accepted in a mere five years. The story is described in the fascinating book *The Golem at Large* by two professors of the sociology of science: Harry Collins and Trevor Pinch.[88]

The challenge facing the AIDS activists could not have been greater. The US gay community had to take on the regulatory authorities of the US Food and Drug Administration (FDA), the medical profession and the intricacies of clinical trial protocols in order to get access to the drugs they needed to stay alive.

Initially there was fear on both sides.

In 1985 William F. Buckley Jr proposed in a notorious *New York Times* piece that "everyone detected with AIDS should be tattooed in the upper forearm to protect common needle users, and on the buttocks, to prevent the victimization of other homosexuals".

Susan Ellenberg, the chief bio-statistician for the trials by the main government body, the National Institute of Allergy and Infectious Diseases (NIAID), said, "… there was this group of guys, and they were wearing muscle shirts, with earrings and funny hair. I was almost afraid. I was really hesitant even to approach them."

The AIDS activists in the group ACT UP were scarcely less afraid of the scientists and the medical jargon. As one San Francisco activist describes the first meeting she attended, "I walked in through the door and it was completely overwhelming, I mean acronyms flying. I didn't know *what* they were talking about."

The secret of the activists' success was that they decided if they were to persuade the establishment how to run their clinical trials better, they would have to learn the language of the scientists and medics.

Many of the activists had no background in science or medicine. For example, Mark Harrington, who later became one of the key activists in New York, had been a script writer. When he realized he needed to learn the language of the scientists, he made a list of all the technical words he needed to understand, which later became a 53-page glossary that was circulated to all the ACT UP group's members.

They used a wide variety of methods to learn the culture and language of the scientists. They attended scientific conferences, learned from sympathetic professionals both inside and outside the movement and read research proposals. They would start with a specific research proposal and work back from that to learn about the drug mechanism and any basic science they needed. Although this was daunting to the activists at first, they found that, just like learning any new language, with perseverance it all became familiar.

This was very effective. Robert Gallo, the co-discoverer of the HIV virus, was initially very dismissive of the activists, but later referred to one of them, Martin Delany, as "one of the most impressive persons I've ever met in my life, bar none, in any field".

They used their expertise to define a clear and credible set of demands. One of these was aimed at making the trials "more humane, relevant and more capable of generating trustworthy conclusions".

In conventional clinical trials, patients are assigned at random to get the active drug or an inactive placebo. The placebo looks just like the real drug, but has no active ingredients, and so allows the researchers to decide whether the results are due to the chemistry of the drug, or just the patients' expectations. This "placebo effect" is very poorly understood but surprisingly important. In some clinical trials, particularly on drugs that act on the brain, the placebo will have almost as strong an effect as the clinically active drug.

Access to the new drug is restricted so that often the only way of getting it is by participating in the trials. However, people with AIDS weren't prepared to accept a 50:50 risk of not getting a potentially lifesaving treatment, just in the cause of science. This meant that people would sign up for the trial, but then would share and swap drugs between themselves to try to ensure that they got at least some of the active drug. They would also open the tablets up so they could taste them and then drop out if they were on the inactive placebo. Even while they were on the trial, often people would continue to use other treatments obtained through the black market. All this made the trials very unreliable.

The activists cleverly didn't try to reject the whole idea of clinical trials, but proposed that patients should be given other ways of obtaining treatment, and so be true volunteers, and that the trials should be "pragmatic" – that is, designed to work in the real world.

The ACT UP group didn't just engage with the scientists in the world of journals and scientific conferences, however, but also practised radical street politics. For example, in autumn 1988 one demonstration outside the first day of classes at Harvard Medical School involved hospital gowns, blindfolds, chains and fake blood sprayed on the pavement.

The combination was very effective. As one leading authority on clinical trials said, "About fifty of them showed up, and took out their watches and dangled them to show that time was ticking away for them... I'd swear that (they) read everything I ever wrote ... and quoted whatever served their purpose. It was quite an experience."

The activists had unique expertise in what would work in the real world, so once a dialogue developed they were genuinely useful to the clinicians in designing the new way of doing trials. They were also uniquely able to explain the pros and cons of particular trials to people with AIDS. However, it was by learning the language of science and by framing their criticisms in the way that scientists could understand that they forced them to respond.

Patient groups and doctors eventually came up with a simple solution. They'd work together to design their own trials, bypassing the bureaucratic delays of the official trials.

One of the first successes was aerosolized pentamidine for treating a form of pneumonia. NIAID had refused to approve it because of lack of evidence for its effectiveness, so community groups in San Francisco and New York decided to test it for themselves without funding or placebos. Nevertheless, in 1989, after carefully examining their data, the FDA approved it: the first time they had approved a drug based purely on community-based research, and a mere five years from the discovery that the HIV virus caused AIDS.

In October 1990 two articles in the *New England Journal of Medicine* detailed the proposed new procedures for clinical trials, and by the next international AIDS conference in June, the activists spoke from the podium rather than shouting from the back of the room.

New ideas must start by being expressed in the language of the old, but one of the dangers is that initially the two groups – the proponents of the new idea and of the old – may be using the vocabulary in different ways. For example, when new age healers talk about "vibrations" they mean something very different from scientists or musicians.

When Copernicus said "the Earth moved", people felt that he was mad. In their terms, they were quite correct to say this, because they were coming from a mental model in which the earth was the centre of the universe. What they meant by Earth was "fixed position". However, Copernicus's vision was not only for a world view in which the Earth went round the sun, but for a whole new way of regarding the problems of physics and astronomy that changed the meanings of both "Earth" and "motion". Without understanding these changes the concept of a moving Earth was indeed mad.

It's often only later in the process that you will be able to sit down together and agree definitions. At this early stage, when you are still trying to overcome people's blindness, it will be up to you to try to understand where they are misunderstanding you, or why they are resisting you, and then to deal with it.

Reframing

Reframing the debate

In late 2000 the Democrats in America were in shock. George Bush had just become president and the Republicans were in charge of virtually everything. Things that were considered extreme a decade ago were now national policy. How could this have happened?

The person who had the best explanation for what was going on was the American psychologist and linguist George Lakoff. His explanation is summarized in an excellent book, *Don't Think of an Elephant: Know Your Values and Reframe the Debate*, which took progressive America by storm.[89]

He points out that people do not vote with their economic self-interest, they vote with their identity and their values. For example, in the 2000 US election Al Gore kept saying that George Bush's tax cuts would only go to the top 1%. Nevertheless, the poorest 99% of conservatives still voted for George Bush because his position fitted with their conservative values, rather than their economic self-interest.

The Democrats lost because they lost control over the language and mental models governing the debate. While they were squabbling over their differences, the radical right and its rich patrons had invested hundreds of millions of dollars over 40 years in supporting think tanks, young talent and spokespeople, and developing communications channels. This transformed the language of American politics.

The language of the right was based around a philosophy of five key concepts: for example, "strong defence" or "family values", which were designed to appeal to the fundamental values of a mental model that many in the USA would call the "strict father morality". This is a mental model based on the idea that the world is a dangerous place, so that what is needed is a strong, strict father who will protect and support the family while teaching his children right from wrong. Sometimes this will require discipline and punishment, but that will be in the child's best interests so that they grow up strong and self-reliant.

This view was sincerely and quite widely held, so was very effective at attracting votes.

In the 2004 State of the Union address, George Bush used a strange phrase. When discussing the international reactions to the operations in Afghanistan and Iraq, he said, "America will never seek a permission slip to defend the security of our country."

Although this phrase seemed puzzling to outsiders, it got applauded by his supporters, because they knew exactly what he meant. Children at school may need to ask the teacher for a permission slip to go to the toilet, but the adult never asks the children for permission. Once you realize that the operating mental model was that America is the adult, surrounded by lesser "child nations" who need to be told what to do and disciplined if they don't do it, the driving principles behind America's foreign policy start to become clear. You still may not think it is right, but it is easier to fight if you understand it.

Some of the language the right used was positively Orwellian. Just as George Orwell's prescient novel *Nineteen Eighty-Four* had the Ministry of Peace, which concerned itself with war, Lakoff pointed out that the US "Clear Skies Act" should really be called the "Dirty Skies Act", because it increases air pollution and mercury poisoning. These sort of misleading names are not confined to the USA. For example, as even the UK's former Health Secretary, Patricia Hewitt, admits, the UK's National Health Service should really be called the National Sickness Service, because it focuses on treating disease rather than on preventing it.[90]

I suspect I am not alone in finding that whenever a supplier tells me that they will be providing an "improved service" my heart sinks, suspecting it's an Orwellian euphemism for higher charges, fewer people and more technology.

Language is powerful, so if you use your opponents' words you just reinforce their mental models. For example, when Richard Nixon said "I am not a crook," everyone thought of him as a crook.

Use of misleading language is often a sign that someone is on weak ground, so if you consistently challenge it and use the more accurate term you will help "reframe the debate". For example, in 2002, the UK government introduced proposals for a national identity card, calling it a "Universal

Entitlement Card" when the true aim was to identify people who were not entitled to benefits. The former editor of the *Daily Telegraph*, Charles Moore, pointed out that this was misleading, Orwellian language: it wasn't providing any entitlements that people didn't already have, and "compulsory" would be a better word than "universal". Everyone continued to talk about ID cards, so the "entitlement" term did not last long; within a year the Home Secretary of the time, David Blunkett, was defending his "Compulsory Identity Card scheme".

As the US conservatives have so successfully demonstrated, taking control of the language is powerful, but to work it must be underpinned by a set of fundamental unifying values. Lakoff therefore calls for the "progressives" in America to define their own values and philosophy and use this to underpin a set of terms with which they can fight back against the right. For example, in place of the conservative concept of "Strong Defence", they might choose "Stronger America". This phrase would give them scope to include the wider dimensions of strength that would appeal to people with a more "nurturant parent" model, who value America's effectiveness and influence in the world, rather than pure military strength, and America's internal strength, such as her economy, educational system, healthcare and environment.

Trigger more useful mental models

Mental models can be very stable and hard to change, but as human beings we are complex and adaptable and so there are often several different mental models that can apply in a given situation. This means that sometimes the best way to get one's idea across is by triggering a more helpful mental model, rather than by attempting to change it.

As Lakoff points out, most Americans have elements of both the "strict father" and the "nurturant parent" models, but may use them in different parts of their lives. If someone was strict in their business life, but compassionate at home, progressives could appeal to them by framing the discussion in terms of their home life, such as secure healthcare for their parents as they age so that they wouldn't have to sell the family home.

Sometimes one can trigger more useful mental models in surprising ways.

The Harvard University social psychologist Professor Teresa Amabile gives a lovely example of a New Yorker who was fed up with kids playing ball against the wall of his apartment. In a stroke of genius, rather than coming out and shouting fruitlessly at them to get them to stop, he offered them ten cents for every ball they kicked against his wall. Pretty soon they lost interest and wandered away.

This might seem a bizarre way of getting them to stop, but as Amabile explains, it worked because by paying them he had triggered a new mental model. The ball game was no longer something they were doing because it was fun, but something that they were being paid to do. Suddenly it began to feel like work, so they lost interest.

We are most creative when we are internally motivated, when we are doing something because it's interesting, fun or feels worthwhile. Artists' non-commissioned work is rated as more creative than their commissioned work. Many people will recognize the difference in how creative you feel when you are at home doing something fulfilling like playing with the kids or cooking dinner for friends, rather than at work, trying to meet an imposed performance target.

Much of Amabile's research has shown that being offered an external reward like money or prizes actually reduces our creativity. This important work suggests that very often when organizations or campaigns try to "incentivize" the behaviour they want by handing out prizes and bonuses, they actually make it less likely the idea will take off. People may well take up the incentives, but their involvement is likely to be more superficial and more easily distracted.

Opening your own eyes

As you will be immersed in your own mental models, it's easy to be blind to the fact that others see things differently. However, by trying to understand their perspective, you can often spot ways to trigger mental models that will make it easier for them to adopt your ideas.

The Housing Department of the UK's Ipswich Borough Council looks after 8,500 homes, rented out to people who need affordable accommodation. As tenants are often on low incomes and are sometimes in difficult circumstances, at any time about 200 tenants a year are at risk of being evicted for non-payment of their rent.

One of the tenancy support workers realized that the people who get into this situation are often not just in a mess with their rent, but also with their income, welfare benefits, healthcare and the justice system.

The staff realized that if they could only teach people to remember their important appointments, it would transform their lives. However, to the staff's surprise they discovered that this wasn't as simple as just giving the tenants a calendar. In contrast to the ordered lives of the council staff, who are mostly working nine to five in secure employment with days dominated by diaries full of appointments and meetings, these tenants' lives have often been in flux since childhood. They are continually battling with an incomprehensible welfare system, a succession of poorly paid temporary jobs and broken promises. Quite understandably, their mental models are ones of randomness and chaos; the concept of calendars and firm appointments doesn't fit with this.

In a simple and clever programme, the housing department manager acquired a selection of nice (but cheap) pictorial calendars and the tenants chose the one they fancied. The tenancy support workers then put in the time to teach them how to use them, explaining that they were like the school timetable: if things are on the timetable, they will definitely happen. The department balanced this framework of order by encouraging the tenants to see the support workers as helpful friends. For example, they started sending text messages instead of formal letters because the tenants saw these as being more interesting and read them.

Dealing with the authorities on the basis that "it's like being at school with a friend" turned out to be a very effective alternative mental model. Within six months, 80% of the tenants on the programme were no longer at risk of eviction. With a little help from the support workers during occasional crises over the next two years, most regained control of their lives and evictions halved within that time.

This example is also a nice illustration of the way that creativity is often motivated by the ability to make a difference, rather than by externally imposed targets. Far from having a target to reduce the number of evictions, the manager only fully realized what a significant improvement the department had made when I started asking for figures.

It is also useful to open our eyes to how easily our own mental models can trick us into jumping to incorrect conclusions. A common one is to assume that people are being wilfully blind to our idea, when in reality the problem is simply that we haven't told them about it.

For example, I watched this happen at one campaign rally where a small dissident group was handing out anonymous leaflets criticizing the policy of the organizers. Unfortunately for them, however, the organizers were so busy they were completely unaware of the leaflets, so the group would have had much more influence if they had had the courage to discuss their views directly.

There are three common reasons why as creative people we assume people are blind, when in reality they are willing to consider our views.

The first is a lack of courage. We assume we'll meet blindness or opposition, but duck out of dealing with it. If we think we've sent someone details of our idea, but hear nothing, it's very easy to jump to the conclusion that they hate it, when the reality may just be that our email didn't arrive, or that they've been too busy to look at it yet.

The second is about our personality. If the personality test in Chapter 2 suggested that we are the Visionary Leader type we may tend to spend too long refining our ideas in private before revealing them.

The final reason may be our inefficiency. Whereas the Careful Conservators and Visionary Leaders tend to be methodical and organized, as Creative Mavericks or Innovative Trouble-Shooters we may be so bound up in developing our ideas that we make a mess of telling people about our ideas: leaving it to the last minute and missing the deadline, putting the wrong address on the envelope or just plain forgetting to tell them.

Priming

The mental model we adopt often depends on our "priming" at any particular moment.

As we saw in the last chapter, our culture has a strong influence on our underlying mental models, but we may have several different competing cultural influences, for example if we were brought up in one culture, but now live and work in another. Quite simple things determine which model is dominant at any time. When bi-cultural students at Hong Kong University were shown pictures that were suggestive of western culture, such as Mickey Mouse, their responses in the experiments that followed were more typically western and individualistic than if they were first primed with "Chinese" pictures like a dragon or a temple.[91] The experimenters explored how the pictures had influenced the students by showing them a cartoon of a fish swimming in front of other fish, and asking the participants why they thought the fish was doing this. The students who saw the American pictures were more likely to give reasons to do with the motivations of the individual fish, while the students who saw the Chinese pictures were more likely to talk about the other fish and the general context. As we saw earlier, this is very consistent with the tendency of eastern cultures to be more sensitive to the overall context and environment, while western ones tend to focus more on the individual.

Even very short exposures can influence our mental models and perceptions. The social psychologist Ulrich Kühnen and colleagues did some remarkable experiments on creating either a collectivist or an independent mindset.[92] Groups of participants were primed by reading a paragraph of text and circling either all the collectivist words like we, us and our, or the individualist ones like I, me and mine. Even this very simple and brief exercise was enough to make a significant difference in how individualist people were in the subsequent exercises.

This priming effect explains why timing and environment are so important in determining whether ideas will get adopted. Ideas for new airport security systems got a lot more attention in the immediate aftermath of 9/11 than they had beforehand.

The environmental organizations Friends of the Earth and Greenpeace have sometimes made best use of a limited advertising budget by using billboard adverts in only one site: outside the offices of the *Guardian* newspaper in London. Although these will be seen by a very small proportion of the UK population, the hope is that the advert will prime the *Guardian*'s journalists, and hence result in better press coverage.

Change their environment

Our mood, the mental models that get triggered, our attention and our responses are all influenced by the environment that we are in.

High-tech entrepreneurs, trying to attract investors and customers, have a choice. In some cases they go for flash premises, creating an environment full of glass, steel and Danish office furniture, to project the impression of success and wealth. Others live in very basic premises, full of mysterious pieces of technical equipment, snaking wires and tottering piles of paper. It's as if they are trying to create an impression of the inventive genius in the garret. I've seen both, and worked in both. Sadly (particularly if you can't afford it), it's much easier to persuade people to spend serious sums of money if you can surround them with an environment that oozes the impression of success and wealth.

If you want someone to adopt a new idea, it helps to invite them out of their customary environment. Getting them out of their office is particularly valuable when dealing with people in slow-moving bureaucracies and rule-bound corporations, where almost any new environment will help them break the patterns of caution and risk aversion. You don't have to have your own office to take them to. One group of cycling campaigners influenced their local city council transport officers very successfully by setting up meetings in a café overlooking a particularly dangerous junction.

Skilled influencers use the environment to make their case much more powerfully than words ever could.

An insightful article in *Harvard Business Review* by W. Chan Kim and Renée Mauborgne describes how Bill Bratton helped turn around the New York Police Department (NYPD).[93] When Bratton took over as commissioner in 1994, the NYPD was an organization that was notoriously difficult to manage. Turf wars were common and crime had become so far out of control that the press referred to the Big Apple as the Rotten Apple. Nevertheless, within two years felony crime fell 37%, murders 50% and theft 35%. The turnaround was often attributed to zero-tolerance policing, but as in all complex human systems, the reality is more complicated. One of the major factors was that Bratton was a superb leader, and very skilled in overcoming complacency.

When he'd first arrived in New York as head of the transit police, he discovered that his senior staff were ignoring the public concern about safety on the subway because only 3% of felony crime happened there. He realized that this was because they all used cars provided by the city, and never travelled on the subway themselves. In order to shake them out of their complacency he ordered that all senior staff, himself included, must travel on the subway to work and to meetings. Very rapidly they realized just how unpleasant an experience it was. Even though few major felonies were committed, the aggressive beggars, homeless (there were 5,000 homeless living in the subway at the time) and gangs of youths jumping turnstiles made it impossible for them to deny that a change was needed.

This approach can also be used with your bosses. Some years earlier, when he'd been running a police division of the Massachusetts Bay Transit Authority (MBTA), the board had decided to buy smaller squad cars. Instead of fighting the decision, Bratton invited the MBTA general manager for a tour of the district. He prepared carefully, using a small car just like the ones that were to be ordered. He jammed the seat forward to demonstrate the leg room for a six-foot policeman, and wore his belt, gun and handcuffs. He then drove the manager over every pothole he could find.

After two hours he'd won his case.

The art of surprise

Mental models are eroded away by an accumulation of examples that don't fit, because they steadily make the existing model seem less useful and appropriate. However, there is a balance to be struck. If the examples are too ordinary and conventional, they will do hardly anything to erode the model. If they are too extreme they will be ignored because they won't fit.

Social psychologists studying the way in which people change their stereotypical views have studied how one can be most effective in helping people change these deep-seated mental models.[94] Their work shows that although it is tempting to try something really dramatic to make people adopt your ideas, dramatic conversions are very rare.

The archetypical story of a dramatic "Road to Damascus" conversion may not even be true. In the Bible, St Luke describes St Paul's conversion on the road to Damascus.[95] An Israelite named Saul (St Paul's original name) had been persecuting the early followers of Jesus and was blinded on the road to Damascus by a flash of light. He heard a voice saying, "Saul, Saul, why do you persecute me?" When he asked who it was, the voice then said, "I am Jesus, who you are persecuting."

For three days Saul was blind and was led by the hand to Damascus. He was only cured when Ananias, a disciple of Jesus, heard a voice telling him to go to the house where Saul was staying and to place his hands on him to restore his sight. When he did this, Saul became able to see again, and was immediately baptized by Ananias.

The phrase "Road to Damascus" has entered the language to describe a sudden conversion, but St Paul's own letters give a more complex and realistic picture than the version in the Bible. For example, as the Pulitzer Prize-winning author and historian Garry Wills points out, Paul himself did not consider his new convictions about Jesus a conversion, but rather part of his ongoing life as a Jew; it was a call, similar to that experienced by the Hebrew prophets, rather than a religious conversion.[96] Wills comments:

> What happened on the Damascus road was that God charged Paul with a message and a mission: Go tell Jews everywhere that the messianic era they had prayed for had dawned and that a certain rabbi from Nazareth, slain by the Romans as a threat to their empire and raised from the dead by God, was the long-anticipated Messiah. Therefore, Paul insisted, the hour had now come – as the prophets had foretold – to welcome the gentiles into the covenant community previously restricted to the seed of Abraham.

It also seems likely that the process of change took rather longer than in St Luke's description. After the baptism St Paul went into the desert, but it was three years before he started his ministry in earnest in Jerusalem. No doubt he'd spent a lot of time thinking in the meantime.

This delay is typical; where dramatic conversions do occur, this is usually because the pre-conversion model is ready to crumble already.

The problem is that isolated or extreme examples are likely to be "sub-typed" and ignored as a special case. People just say, "It's the exception that proves the rule."

When police liaison offices were introduced into a secondary school in an attempt to improve students' views of the police, the students decided that the liaison officers were better than most police, but didn't change their view about police in general.[97]

There are two aspects that determine whether someone is sub-typed and ignored. The first, and most important factor, is how representative the person is of the stereotype; the second factor is about what they do to "disconfirm" the stereotype.

Disconfirming examples have more impact if they come from someone who is reasonably representative of the group, rather than someone who looks like an outsider. The more unrepresentative they look, the more likely they are to be sub-typed as an exception and ignored.

To broaden the views of someone who thinks that lawyers are grasping, bring along someone who looks and sounds like a stereotypical lawyer but is doing something that will contradict their stereotype, such as working on human rights for a pittance. If you bring along a human rights lawyer wearing jeans and with a ponytail, they are more likely to be ignored as an exception.

This principle has important implications for getting your idea across. If your ideas are being resisted, it is tempting to dress and act in a dramatic way to try to break through the resistance. However, the sub-typing effect means that although this may get you noticed, your ideas will then be much more likely to be ignored. It's much more effective to try to look as if you fit in, making your ideas and actions provide the drama.

Combine the familiar with the exceptional

Sometimes opening people's eyes will take a team effort, with some people providing the "disconfirming" drama, while other, more conventional-looking supporters provide a way for the audience to empathize and connect.

In the 1990s a massive expansion in the roads-building programme in the UK spawned a vigorous anti-roads protest movement. Although in virtually all cases the protesters lost their individual battles and the individual roads went ahead, both the pro-roads lobby and the environmentalists agree that overall the succession of "noisy defeats and quiet victories" got the issue recognized and resulted in a substantial reduction in the roads-building programme for the next decade. Of the 600 roads schemes planned in 1989, 500 had been scrapped by 1997. The road building budget halved for the next decade.

The Newbury Bypass protests were characterized by direct action, in which protesters set up camp in trees and later built tunnels in the path of the road. Others chained themselves to equipment. As the photograph at the start of this chapter shows, the contractor had to use professional climbers to remove protesters from trees. Running in parallel with this, there was a much more conventional campaign using various legal, political and media tactics.

In a thoughtful commentary on the lessons learned, one of the direct-action campaigners of the Newbury Bypass protests points out that although the spectacular direct action was vital for getting media attention, the protesters themselves became stereotyped and hence their ideas were ignored.[98] He said:

> *This media and cultural focus on protester lifestyles and spectacular tactics helps to alienate many people from our struggles, to stereotype activists, and thus to fit the movement into a pigeonhole (or perhaps a tunnel?). Everyone's heard of Swampy, but few know what he was digging under, or why, or could relate this to their own lives.[99]*

The protests were successful in their overall goal of reducing road building, in large part because of the power of using different tactics simultaneously. For example, another campaign aimed to stop the expansion of a proposed quarry in the southwest of England, which had been given planning permission despite years of campaigning by the local parish council. It had basically been ignored, until the site was occupied by a couple of activists and it suddenly became headline news. This then allowed the campaigners to restart the conventional campaign and rapidly collect 3,000 signatures against the scheme. Commenting on why it worked, the same anonymous campaigner said:

> *A whole suite of traditional campaigning techniques – legal, media, and political – were then applied in tandem with direct action and the scheme was rapidly booted out to a public inquiry (which would never have happened if the local people had used traditional techniques alone). This is the best way to use direct action. It's all about teamwork ... using all the tools together.*

This combination of the conventional and the radical is a powerful way to open people's eyes to your ideas, whether it's a campaign or an invention.

In 1963 Richard Moog invented the first commercial electronic music synthesizer, the Moog Synthesizer. Synthesizers were large and complex machines, but were only designed for use in studios. A few rock musicians and experimental classical composers had made recordings, but the first big hit was Wendy Carlos's *Switched-On Bach* in 1968. This was an album of ten of Bach's best-known pieces, ranging from "Air on a G string" to Brandenburg Concerto no. 3. As the early synthesizer could only play one note at a time, Carlos had to record each part separately on a custom eight-track tape machine before transferring them to a master tape. The laborious process took months but the results were remarkable. As Richard Moog said, "This was a seminal record because up until then people were more familiar with the synthesizer as a device that made funny sounds, unusual sounds, novelty sounds. The conventional wisdom going into 1968 was that you couldn't use it for real music. Carlos proved that wrong with *Switched-On Bach*."[100]

The album was released to critical derision, largely because the classical music critics felt it trivialized the work of the great composer, but it went on to become the best-selling classical record ever, won several Grammy awards and became the first classical album to go platinum.[101]

Subsequently Moog developed the much easier to use Minimoog, and soon many musicians and groups, including the Doors, the Grateful Dead, the Rolling Stones and the Beatles were using Moog synthesizers. The boom times didn't last for Moog, however, and by 1971 a combination of competition from other manufacturers and declining interest in electronic music meant that his business ran out of money and he had to sell the controlling interest. In 2002, after a long legal battle, Moog recovered the right to the Moog brand, and was once again able to sell instruments bearing his name.

Exploiting the unexpected

Sometimes we can develop a demonstration of our ideas that will run as we'd hoped. However, all too frequently, our efforts will be eclipsed by external events that are out of our control. Many of these will be unexpected and unplanned, and may well be far more dramatic than anything we could have arranged ourselves. These external events may be disruptive, or they may be helpful.

As Harold Macmillan, UK prime minister from 1957 to 1963, said when asked by a young journalist after a long dinner what can most easily steer a government off course, "Events, dear boy. Events."

Politicians have to cope with the unpredictable, and so do we when we're trying to get our ideas adopted. Often these unexpected events will just be a distraction, as people quite understandably pay attention to dealing with them, rather than listening to our bright idea.

However, if our idea is trying to address a slowly developing problem, some of these unexpected events will be caused by the problem we are trying to solve and will therefore give us an opportunity. If we are trying to persuade our employer to improve its creaking IT infrastructure, a major system crash may be unwelcome, but will at least open people's eyes to the need for a solution ... if we play it right.

As we'll see in more detail later, people have been very slow in paying serious attention to climate change. There are many reasons for this, but one is that, on a human timeframe, the changes have been happening slowly. However, sudden events like the catastrophe in New Orleans following Hurricane Katrina acted as a huge wakeup call to the US public.[102]

This could easily have been ignored as disconnected with climate change, except for the publication of two influential scientific reports in the weeks before. These showed that the rising sea surface temperatures were increasing the destructive power of hurricanes. When the catastrophe happened, people wanted to understand why, and the scientific reports were picked up by the media and NGO commentators.[103]

To exploit events successfully, you need to connect the event to your issue, and do it quickly and clearly, but avoid exploiting the suffering of the people affected by the immediate crisis. If you get it wrong you will be heavily criticised, in the same way that the UK government special adviser Jo Moore caused understandable outrage (and was ultimately forced to resign) for sending an email to her department head as the twin towers burned on 11 September 2001, saying, "It's now a very good day to get out anything we want to bury."

Avoiding misinterpretation

It's very tempting to try to open people's eyes by doing something so dramatic that people can't ignore it. Unfortunately, however, people will be remarkably good at misinterpreting your dramatic demonstration.

If they can, they will force-fit it into their existing mental models. For example, as the American journalist Mark Kurlansky points out, the Romans crucified Jesus hoping that the humiliation and death of the Christians' leader would put an end to the dangerous idea of Christianity.[104] They could hardly have expected that his followers would then insist that he had died forgiving his torturers, and would adopt the crucifix as their symbol.

Where different groups have different mental models, this means that they may well interpret events in radically different ways. In April 2007, following the tragic shooting of 32 students and staff at Virginia Tech by Cho Seung-Hui, UK commentators used it to illustrate the dangers of easy access to guns. In the USA, the National Rifle Association used it to argue for even wider gun ownership (on the basis that this would have allowed the students and professors to have protected themselves).

An effect called the Fundamental Attribution Error means that people can also be remarkably obtuse about deciding that your demonstration is due to personal factors, rather than the reality of the situation.[105] For example, if you decide that the time has come to make a dramatic scene about the deteriorating facilities at your golf course, for which members are being charged a small fortune, you may find that the committee wildly misinterprets the reasons for your action. Instead of recognizing that you are making a fuss because the facilities genuinely need improving, they may well put it down to your personality or attitudes, deciding for example that you are playing politics or in financial difficulties over your membership dues.

You will need to be very careful if your audience is to interpret your dramatic demonstration in the way that you want.

"Go all the way"

In 1884 the great British engineer and inventor Charles Parsons (founder of my first employer, C. A. Parsons) invented the modern steam turbine. He realized that it would be ideal both for electrical power generation and for ship propulsion, because both needed high efficiency and had a steady demand for power.

At the time, power generators were driven by reciprocating steam engines, so, as might be expected, his idea of using steam to drive a rotating turbine was so radical that it was resisted. Interestingly, however, after an initial period of frustration, he used two quite different methods for getting his turbine adopted in the two different markets, ships and electrical power generation.

In 1889 he set up his own company in Newcastle-upon-Tyne, in the northeast of England, to develop and manufacture the new steam turbine. This was a significant technical challenge because everything about the design was new and had to be invented. Even today, manufacturing turbine blades is hard because of the complicated shapes and the precision needed, but he also had to develop an electric generator to be driven by the turbine. This was not easy because electro-magnetism was still poorly understood and it was several years before the establishment of the fundamental principles of how to design electrical machines.

He had a few customers for his turbine for use in lighting on ships, but had great difficulty getting the new land-based electric-lighting companies interested. Sceptics questioned whether it would ever be sufficiently reliable for large-scale power generation. He decided he would have to kick start the process himself, so in 1890 he got together with friends to set up the New-castle and District Electric Lighting Co., installing a pair of his new turbo-generators in the Forth Banks Power Station. By 1892 he had units producing a very useful 100kW and had backed another demonstration power plant in Cambridge but still had no power-station customers.

He decided to build a boat to demonstrate the turbine's potential. Two years later he took out a patent for a steam-turbine-powered vessel and set up a second company to focus on the development of the marine turbine.

After initial experiments with models, he built the *Turbinia*. In a revolu-tionary design, this was 30.5 m long and only 2.7 m wide. Although perform-ance in the initial experiments was disappointing, after meticulous observation and experiments he then changed the design so that the steam passed through

Turbinia at speed in the North Sea   Photograph by Alfred J. West, FRGS © Birr Castle Archives

three turbines in succession, powering nine propellers on three separate shafts. This resulted in a top speed of 34.5 knots, about 4 knots faster than the fastest destroyers then afloat.

The initial sea trials took place off the coast of northeast England. *Turbinia* was spectacularly fast, but cramped, hot, noisy and decidedly wet. Other vessels reporting on the high-speed runs observed that all they saw of *Turbinia* was "a bow emerging from a huge wave and a flame from the funnel flickering into the air".

Charles Parsons once wrote, "If you believe in a principle, never damage it with a poor impression. You must go all the way."

He decided to make a dramatic demonstration.

On 16 June 1897 he brought the *Turbinia*, uninvited, to the Navy Review for the sixtieth anniversary of Queen Victoria's accession to the throne. This was the greatest armada the world had seen, with 165 ships from the Royal Navy alone, manned by 38,000 men. All, except for six sailing brigs, were powered with reciprocating engines. The review was watched by the Queen, the Prince of Wales and Prince Heinrich of Prussia, brother of the German Kaiser, and assembled foreign dignitaries.

Just as the national anthem started up, the *Turbinia* darted out and sped past the line of ships. A patrol boat was sent after her, but the *Turbinia* was so fast she could not be caught and her wash nearly sank her pursuer.

Parsons cut it fine, nearly hitting a French yacht, but the spectacular demonstration worked. The British Admiralty could no longer afford to ignore the turbine. The following year the Admiralty placed its first order for a turbine-powered torpedo boat, although it insisted that Parsons put down a £100,000 deposit in case it did not perform to its specifications. By 1914 all the Royal Navy's most important ships were powered by Parsons' steam turbines.

It is often assumed that the Admiralty was scandalized, but a few at the British Navy had been interested in his work for a while. The Director of Naval Construction at the British Admiralty, Sir William White, kept a keen eye on the new developments and visited the ship during a refit in 1897. It has also been suggested that Sir John Durston, the Engineer-in-Chief of the Royal Navy, had encouraged Parsons. However, as so often happens, even senior insiders couldn't persuade a conservative organization like the British Admiralty to adopt a new technology; it needed a shock to the system to open people's eyes to the need for change.

Spreading out your evidence

As Parsons' experience with the *Turbinia* shows, a dramatic demonstration of your ideas can work, if you have the courage to "go all the way", particularly if you can attract some internal supporters who will help make sure it's interpreted in the right way. There is, however, an alternative, quieter approach that can be even more effective than the dramatic demonstration: spreading out your evidence.

This was explored by the social psychologists Renée Weber and Jennifer Crocker, who were interested in how to change people's stereotypical views about people of different races, sexes or religions – something that's normally very hard to do.[106] In their experiments, they took undergraduates from Northwestern University in Illinois and, rather than dealing with something as sensitive as race, looked at what techniques worked best for changing their views of different professions, for example, corporate lawyers.

Their results showed that the most effective way to make people change their minds was to spread the available evidence out, providing as many examples as possible, each of which contradicted the stereotype in a different way. This could be much more effective than "going for it" and piling all the evidence into a single dramatic example.

It was important that each example was dramatic enough, however, because examples that were only a little bit unusual weren't enough to contribute to budging the stereotype. If people were uncertain of what they thought corporate lawyers were like, or realized that they would not all be the same, the examples needed to be more dramatic in order to get over the threshold that would stimulate change.

The Intergovernmental Panel on Climate Change (IPCC) seemed to have been following this approach very successfully throughout 2007 when it released the reports of its three working party groups separately: "Science" in February, "Impacts" in April, and "Options" in May, followed by the full "Assessment Report" later in the year. This got much more attention, and had much more influence than if all the information had all been released simultaneously.

Parsons also adopted this approach with his turbo-generator. *Turbinia* had been very successful in selling the concept of the steam turbine to the Navy, but the dramatic demonstration had little impact on the electrical-power-generation business. In contrast to the noisy *Turbinia*, one of the main initial advantages of Parson's turbo-generators was that they were so much quieter than the thumping reciprocating engines.

He therefore focused his efforts on a succession of demonstrations round the country. Orders picked up dramatically after he saved the chief London power station of the Metropolitan Electric Supply Co. from being shut down. It was under threat because of complaints about the public nuisance caused by the noisy reciprocating engines driving the generators, so Parsons' much quieter turbo-generators were a great advantage.

In 1894 he told his brother Laurence that he had more orders than he could cope with, and by 1896, the year before the sensational demonstration of the *Turbinia*, Parsons had licensed the American rights to the turbo-generator to the American entrepreneur, Westinghouse. Over the years the size and power of the turbo-generators steadily increased, and as they did so their advantages became more and more obvious.

By the time of his death in 1931, Charles Parsons had the satisfaction of seeing his invention adopted by all of the world's major power stations. Even today, the massive 660MW turbo-generator sets used in power stations all around the world are the direct descendant of his designs: a credit to his skill and creativity as an engineer, but also to his skill and persistence in getting attention paid to his ideas.

6

Frozen

"It's not worth it"

In the second stage, people are at least aware of the idea you are trying to get them to adopt. However, even though their eyes are now open to it, all too often they come up with all sorts of excuses about why it's not worth paying it serious attention.

They say things like, "The data's unconvincing"; "It's too risky, too expensive"; "The effect will be insignificant"; "It's someone else's responsibility"; or "I have more important priorities".

It gets very frustrating, and they often seem to be deliberately trying to demotivate you.

There may be an element of truth in all these statements, of course, so it's important not to totally ignore them, but the excuses are also a symptom that the recipient is "frozen". They are aware of the idea, but insufficiently motivated to do anything about it, even if logically it's obvious that they should.

They are like rabbits frozen in the headlights of an approaching car.

This chapter focuses on how to help people face up to uncomfortable and significant ideas. These are particularly likely to make people freeze up, because uncomfortable ideas tend to trigger people's defences, while significant ideas almost always demand a level of emotional commitment, time and energy that people are initially reluctant to give.

They will only unfreeze and be willing to accept new ideas if it becomes incontrovertibly clear that something they care about needs to change and they feel safe enough to admit it.

Frozen in the headlights

The classic example of people being frozen into inaction about an unwelcome idea is the threat of climate change.

Scientists have been aware of the threat for a surprisingly long time, although initially they were blind to the danger. At the end of the nineteenth century, the Swedish chemist and Nobel Prize-winner Svante Arrhenius got interested in the causes of the ice ages, and set himself the task of calculating how much water vapour and carbon dioxide, CO_2, warmed the earth. By 1896 he had calculated that doubling the CO_2 level would increase average global temperatures by 5–6°C. This was slightly higher than today's estimate of about 3°C, but still a remarkably accurate estimate for the time.[107] He was aware that coal-burning was pumping CO_2 into the atmosphere, but was unconcerned because he calculated that it would take 3,000 years to increase CO_2 levels by half. However, fossil-fuel use increased far faster than he expected, so that by the turn of the 21st century, CO_2 levels were already 30% higher than a hundred years earlier: far higher than at any time in over 650,000 years.

There has been scientific consensus that global warming is real and largely human-induced since 1993, and temperature rises of 2–3°C are now thought likely within the next fifty years.

This is a very unwelcome idea, because the consequences of a few degrees rise are frightening. Hundreds of millions, if not billions, of people will face being driven from their homes by extreme weather events, sea level rise, starvation as crops fail and water shortages as vital glaciers disappear. The UK's Stern Review Report calculated in 2006 that if we continue "business as usual" it could cost 5–20% of GDP.[108]

The upside is that there are also lots of things we can do to help prevent the most serious effects, and that prevention is expected to cost substantially less than the damage from doing nothing.[109] The problem is that, as George Bush said in January 2006, "America is addicted to oil,"[110] and much of the rest of the developed world is in a similar situation.

The sense of fear and helplessness is triggering all the typical "frozen" reactions to an unwelcome idea. Almost everybody can claim that it's not worth taking action because they are only a small part of the problem. For some reason it seems particularly popular to claim that you are only 2% of the problem, as did Airbus on behalf of the aviation sector in 2006[111] and Tony Blair on behalf of the whole of the UK in 2007.[112] Others try to deny the need to do anything about it, so initially sceptics questioned the reality of climate change, then questioned that it was human induced. By 2000 many admitted that it was happening, but argued that there are still too many uncertainties to do anything about it[113] or that it was uneconomic to deal with it[114] or that we should just live with the consequences. More recently this defence has also started to crumble, but people defend themselves from accepting the need to make personal changes to their lifestyle by arguing that technology or carbon trading will solve it instead.

Even people who fully accept the scale of the problem and the need for personal action can still be frozen when it comes to actually making difficult personal changes themselves. In early 2006, Tony Wheeler, founder of Lonely Planet travel books, started encouraging his readers to fly less to help prevent climate change. However, when asked about his own flights, he says, "I'm not going to stop, but every time I jump on a plane I think, 'Oh no, I'm doing it again'."[115]

Many environmentalists would recognize these feelings of guilt and paralysis: switching to low energy light bulbs is one thing, negotiating with the family to change holiday plans is harder.

As is so often the case when trying to get difficult ideas adopted, this sort of internal contradiction is normal. It's also typical that different people are at very different stages of acceptance. While some are still blind to the issue, others are aware of it, but frozen in denial or inaction. Others have moved through these stages, and are actively exploring the business opportunities in a low-carbon economy, or the potential for a better, cleaner lifestyle. Understandably, many people are confused by all the different voices clamouring for attention on the issue, so do nothing.

Increasingly around the turn of the century, various UK government agencies and NGOs were trying to persuade people to change their attitudes and behaviours about climate change, but with little success. No matter how much information was made available about ways to improve energy efficiency, no one was really interested: the low cost of energy meant that there was no economic imperative and somehow the threats of global catastrophe didn't seem to connect with daily life. By the early years of the 21st century, both governments and NGOs recognized that a new tack was needed. As the communications agency Futura, who were commissioned by DEFRA (the Department for Environment, Food and Rural Affairs) to look at the problem for the UK government, said, "It's not like selling a particular brand of soap – it's like convincing someone to use soap in the first place."[116]

Traditionally, environmental messages tended to be doom laden and the solutions simple, along the lines of "send £25 and save the rainforest". However, if they are to persuade us to change ourselves, rather than just stimulate us to send off a cheque, climate change communications need to tread the difficult line between triggering denial and despair. For example, they need to wake us up by being clear about the urgency and human consequences of climate change (so that we care), but then find ways of making the solutions feel achievable, attractive and equal to the scale of the problem (to help us feel ready to take action).

This reanalysis, from many sources, is leading to a profound change in the tone of UK climate campaigns. They are moving from being apocalyptic towards being much more positive and aspirational in tone, for example the campaigns of the Stop Climate Chaos coalition.[117] There is also much more emphasis on encouraging a sense of collective action, in both local community groups and national campaigns. For example, the Stop Climate Chaos coalition was founded in 2005, bringing together the millions of members of membership-based NGOs to create a public mandate for political action. Similarly in April 2007, eight major UK companies set up a coalition and launched a campaign entitled "We're in This Together" aiming to engage their millions of customers. Other similar coalitions are growing rapidly round the world in all sorts of sectors, for example the US-based Alliance for Climate Protection, set up by former Vice President Al Gore.

Climate change is a serious global issue, and one on which it's genuinely easy to feel inadequate. However, we are often frozen about accepting unwelcome ideas, even when resolving the problem is clearly under our direct personal control.

One of the biggest problems in research and development is stopping unsuccessful projects. Reminiscent of the un-killable living dead, these are often called "zombie" projects. There may well be clear evidence that the new product doesn't work well enough, or that the customers are unlikely to buy it. Nevertheless, the project rolls on because everyone keeps hoping that just one more tweak will make it all work out OK.

One of the most notable "zombie" projects I worked on was Sir Clive Sinclair's C5. Although the basic idea of a low-cost, open-top electric vehicle was

Sir Clive Sinclair's unusual C5 electric vehicle, with the inventor driving it   Getty Images

a good one, the resulting product was a disaster. It was a three wheeler, powered by a washing machine motor and had a maximum speed of 15 mph. It was much slower on hills, but even though it had been given pedals so the driver could help keep it moving, it was so heavy that these were virtually useless.

The second problem was the unusual driving position, which made you feel ridiculous. To drive it, you sat in a reclining position, with your knees in the air, steering with a bar under your knees. This made it distinctly embarrassing to drive if wearing a skirt, which was a pity as its dismal performance meant that the most likely customers were elderly ladies, even though it had been given a go-faster stripe down the side in an attempt to make it appeal to youngsters.

You also needed to feel courageous to drive it in traffic, as it was so tiny that your nose was at the level of the exhaust from the passing trucks and you felt virtually invisible.

Virtually everyone on the project team had serious doubts about it, but nevertheless it went ahead and was launched with great fanfare in January 1985. I'm not sure why this date was chosen, but the middle of the British winter was a strangely arrogant time to launch an open-topped vehicle. Although it had been designed to sell in the tens of thousands, only about five hundred were ever sold.

In retrospect, one of the key (unnoticed) warning signs that it was heading for disaster was the culture in which people were told, "Don't say this is stupid, just try and find a way of doing it."

I was told this in relation to the tiny part of the system that I was designing, but, as is so common, this cultural attitude was reflected all the way up and down the organization. We were all frozen in denial, hoping our hard work would all pay off in the end.

Why do people freeze up about new ideas?

The basic reason why people so often freeze up when they are faced with a significant new idea is very simple: the pressure to do something is perfectly balanced by their internal resistance to doing anything. In other words, the expected gain (from relieving the pressure) doesn't seem worth the cost.

The benefit is all too often very vague and uncertain, but the costs of exploring and adopting a new idea are only too clear, at least to the recipient.

Some of the costs of adopting a new idea are because of the psychological investment we have made in the previous way of doing things. In theory this shouldn't matter, but if someone has just spent a lot of money on a new car, they are likely to be quite resistant to the idea that they should have bought a different model.

In the 1970s, Steve Sasson invented digital photography at Kodak, but his ideas were spurned. Even in the 1990s, Kodak remained blind to the idea that customers might prefer digital to film cameras, because their mental models about what customers wanted were all about film quality: colour balance, stability, grain size and sensitivity. They made excellent film, but this made it hard for them to realize that most people would happily sacrifice picture quality if they could see their pictures immediately, adjust mistakes and delete the rubbish. Even when they were aware that there was a growing trend to digital photography, it was hard for Kodak to bring themselves to switch over because they had a very successful business, built on decades of investment in film manufacturing, processing and distribution. On the other hand, they knew very little about how to make money out of digital photography, and so would be likely to be in a weak position. Finally, very late in the day, the evidence became so overwhelming that they were forced to restructure the business. This was painful, but by 2007 it was looking as if they'd survive. And Steve Sasson, still at Kodak, was named in the prestigious Consumer Electronics Hall of Fame.

Our perception of the costs of adopting a new idea doesn't just apply to tangible, calculable things, like the investments we need to make in order to exploit it, but also to deeper personal issues. We ignore these at our peril.

Firstly, there is the time taken to understand it. This can be significant if someone has the Careful Conservator personality type and so likes to explore things carefully and in detail. If the idea is a significant one, adopting it will disrupt a range of important mental models, so it will take the recipient a lot of effort to adopt and integrate it.

Secondly, it has psychological costs. For example, it may involve admitting that something is going wrong. This may result in an embarrassing loss of "face", particularly if someone has gone public in opposition to the idea, or it may stir up painful emotions that they'd rather ignore. The cognitive-dissonance effect means that it is very stressful to realize that important beliefs, actions or attitudes are incompatible with each other. This tension can be a great source of creativity in finding a way to resolve the conflict, but it can also drive people to create bizarre reasons to explain away the conflict. If the new idea conflicts with one of their ideas, their natural emotional attachment to it will make them reluctant to switch allegiance.

Finally, learning to do anything new tends to stir up anxiety, so there is also the fear of looking (or being) incompetent while learning the new way of doing things.

Understandably, people will not see why they should embark on all this effort and personal pain when our idea might or might not ultimately be beneficial after all, so they start raising objections that will give them an excuse for their inaction.

Once we realize that this is what is happening, rather than being distracted by trying to solve the specific objections they've raised, we can recognize that the excuses are symptoms that they are frozen, and can focus our efforts on trying to deal with the underlying problem. If we can create a motivation and readiness to change, we will then be able to engage their creativity to help us make our idea real.

The unfreezing process

The first principle is that it's not enough just to provide data and facts. To motivate people to explore our ideas we need to make the personal psychological benefit greater than the cost.

The second principle is that the easiest way to deal with the resistance to a new idea is to try to deflate the resistance, rather than overcome it. This is much more effective than *just* attempting to build up the pressure for change, because when we feel under attack we defend ourselves, stop listening and resist new ideas even more strongly. It's only when we feel sufficiently psychologically safe that we relax and become open to new ideas.

The eminent organizational psychologist Edgar Schein points out that people will unfreeze if we do three things simultaneously.[118]

a) Provide clear evidence that the current situation is no longer OK. (Schein refers to this as providing "disconfirmation".)

b) Make them care.

c) Make it psychologically safe to care.

The first two elements increase the personal pressure by providing undeniable evidence that something they care about is going wrong. The third element, psychological safety, provides the relief valve. Without this, the rising stress level may well just paralyze people with fear or indecision, or trigger all sorts of unhelpful defence mechanisms. These can range from active resistance to the idea to bizarre and virtually unconscious psychological defences that are designed to protect someone from unbearably painful emotions.

For example, one chief executive I worked with blamed his managers for being poor at communicating his visionary ideas down the organization. This was a comfortable, although unfair belief that let him protect himself from the more painful personal realization that it was his own lack of communication skills that was the source of the problem.

Only when all three elements are in place will people feel motivated and safe enough to unfreeze and be ready to seriously consider our idea.

We can recognize the impact of the unfreezing process at work in ourselves.

If the boss tells us off in public for doing a bad job, it's very easy to come away saying to our friends, "She was in a bad mood today," ignoring what she had to say. If, on the other hand, she had started by quietly and privately letting us see just how much our mistake had hurt our colleagues and friends, we would be mortified. By creating a supportive atmosphere, probing us about what went wrong and listening to our answers she would provide the safety for us to relax our defences and start actively looking for ideas about how to do better next time.

The following sections give various examples of ways of providing these three elements – the evidence, concern and safety that will unfreeze people about your idea – but it's important to remember that you need to do all three simultaneously, not in sequence.

Providing clear evidence

To start to unfreeze people the evidence needs to be strong, clear and very relevant to their concerns. It usually needs to give them a shock.

It took a catastrophic accident like the explosion of the space shuttle *Challenger* to wake up NASA to the true risks involved in launching the shuttle. Before the accident, the top management believed that there was a one in 100,000 chance of failure. After the disaster it was recognized that it was about one in fifty, an estimate that looks pretty accurate, given that by 2007 there had been 115 launches and two catastrophic failures. Interestingly, this is a little worse than the one in 100 estimated by the engineers that worked on the booster rocket, but every layer of management had rounded it up before reporting it on upwards.[119]

Threats are very often good ways of getting people's attention. The most obvious are physical or financial threats to the group's survival or wellbeing, for example, an accident, bankruptcy or legal scandal. However, they can also include political, moral or internal threats – a rival will get ahead (a political threat), you will be seen as selfish or irresponsible (a moral threat) or you will fail to live up to your own goals and ideals (an internal threat).

In an ideal world people would all be receptive to bad news and immediately spring into action to deal with the threat, but unfortunately the reality is that all sorts of other less-helpful responses are often easier. As a result they deny the problem, shoot the messenger and ignore the message.

This means that you need to think carefully about how to provide your evidence in the most effective way, so that it is powerful and helps motivate the recipient's desire for a new approach without increasing their psychological resistance to doing anything about it.

Clear messages

The first thing is that evidence needs to be clear if it is to unfreeze people.

When Merck developed the first practical anti-cholesterol drug, Mevacor, a key element of their marketing strategy was to publicize an obscure Finnish study showing a link between high cholesterol levels and heart disease. This made family doctors concerned to reduce their patients' cholesterol levels. Whereas in the past the treatment for high cholesterol had been very unpleasant, Mevacor was a simple tablet, so it provided the doctors with the obvious way to deal with their concern.

Because it provided family doctors with clear evidence (cholesterol mattered), connection (they cared about their patient's health) and safety (a clear action to take), it was a very successful marketing tactic. Interestingly, this was effective even though Merck showed no evidence that reducing cholesterol levels would reduce heart disease.

Often the reality is more complex than the message. Dietary advice has emphasized the risk of saturated fats for 30 years. Certainly the Finnish diet of the time had very high levels of saturated fat and it was assumed that the fat levels had caused the high rate of heart disease in the study. However, more recent research suggests that it's very hard to change your cholesterol levels by changing your diet.[120] In an extreme example of this, the Swedish researcher Fredrik Nyström replicated Morgan Spurlock's film *Super Size Me* under laboratory conditions.[121] He recruited 18 volunteer student subjects, who spent a month on a diet of junk food that gave them double their normal calorie intake. Although some gained 15% of their body weight in just a few weeks, others gained very little. Surprisingly, even though they were on a diet high in saturated fat, many of them showed very little change in their cholesterol levels.

Merck's campaign worked because it had a powerful message that was simple and believable, glossing over the complexities.

The respected former Greenpeace campaign manager Chris Rose points out that campaigning is not the same as education.[122] Although explaining the complexities is good in an educational setting, it also causes confusion and this can paralyze people. Good campaigns have a clear and simple message, hopefully one that is grounded in truth, for example, "High cholesterol is killing your patients", "Lead in petrol gives kids brain damage" or "Dyson vacuum cleaners suck better because there's no bag to clog".

These were all very successful messages.

Ask questions

It's important for the evidence to be direct and clear to start the unfreezing process, but the problem is that if you just jump in and tell someone highly unwelcome information, they are likely to just increase the strength of their denials and defences.

One good way around this problem is to quietly ask good questions and start a dialogue. These questions can be of two types: open or closed. Both can be very useful but serve different functions.

Open questions invite a long answer, and so are often of the form, "What do you think of my idea?" or "How are the problems affecting you?"

When using open questions you let the respondent take control, encouraging them to think and reflect. This can be very effective in engaging people, but the lack of control can feel alarming, so we often use them much less than we should.

Closed questions invite a very short answer (often just a yes or a no) to a very specific issue, such as "Do you want to hear more about my idea?" or "How much does this problem cost you per year?"

When using closed questions you keep control, so they can be good for focusing the discussion in on the topics that you want to cover or delivering a knockout blow. The danger is that because the answers are so short, you still end up doing all the talking. If you get a "no" to a question like, "Do you want to know more?", you are also a bit stuck!

It's not always easy to find the right questions, because to work they must be important to the person you are trying to influence, and ones which will move them closer to adopting your ideas. However, if you can find these questions, it can be transformational. I was once working with a company where there was a widespread belief amongst the engineers that if you showed initiative and "stuck your head above the parapet" you would be fired. Unsurprisingly, this was seriously damaging their creativity, which was why I had been brought in. On discussing the issue with the company's human resources director it became very clear that he felt that the staff turnover of 10–20% every year was healthy.

He and I had very different backgrounds and hence very different mental models about how to motivate people. Arguing my point of view would just have reinforced our differences, so I changed tack. While packing up to go, out of interest rather than any grand plan, I asked him how many people he had made redundant in his career. To my amazement he said, "One hundred thousand." I asked him quietly, "Is that what you want on your tombstone?" He blurted out, "Good God, no," and we finished the interview. My question clearly affected him deeply, because a few days later one of his senior colleagues who knew I'd been meeting with him said, "I don't know what you did, Anne, but Ralph [not his real name] has completely changed."

Questions are good because you don't have to know all of the answers yourself and you don't have to force people to do things. You just need to stimulate the right people to get to work on the right question.

In this case, Ralph was very experienced, so I felt confident that if I could only open his eyes to the problem he would come up with a good solution to it.

Asking carefully chosen open questions is also a good way to gather allies who will in turn ask questions and help you unfreeze the recipients of your idea. For example, a scientist in a high-tech company was becoming increasingly frustrated at the amount of management information that was archived or sent around on paper rather than electronically.

The paper archive was incomplete and hard to access, important information arrived days or even weeks after it was needed, and distributing it made unnecessary work for the support staff. As it was the time of year for budgeting for capital expenditure, the scientist had initially planned to submit a request for the software package he thought would do the job. However, as he and I discussed it, it became clear that the management must have been very aware of the problem for a while, so probably needed unfreezing first.

He therefore decided to start by going around and asking questions to understand why it was done the way it was, where the likely resistance would be and who else would be on his side in calling for change. He also started gathering some punchy examples of how much money the mistakes caused by the paper system had cost the company (for example a business contract a team had lost because they were unaware of expertise in a different part of the building). He could then use these to contradict the management's idea that the current situation was OK.

As so often happens, asking questions often reveals surprising information. He had noticed that files at the end of the alphabet seemed particularly difficult to access. When he investigated, it turned out that this was because the filing clerk was scared of the spiders at the far end of the filing room. This aspect of the problem was solved just by sending in the cleaners!

Apply pressure from different directions

It may be possible to ignore one inconvenient piece of information, but it is much more difficult when evidence is coming at you from all directions. This is because, as we saw in the last chapter, people are more likely to change their minds if they are faced with a number of examples that contradict their expectations, rather than just one.

Ideas are not adopted (or developed) in isolation, but are influenced by the society in which they exist. This gives them their context and often determines how and when they will get adopted.

As the eminent philosopher and historian of science Thomas Kuhn pointed out, most scientific revolutions come about because of "the persistent failure of the puzzles of normal science to come out as they should".[123] It's not enough just for there to be a problem with one area, or for the problems to be in an obscure area that the scientific community is not concerned about. There needs to be "a period of pronounced professional insecurity" to motivate the change.

For example, when in 1543 Copernicus's revolutionary "heliocentric" idea that the earth went round the sun was finally published in his *De revolutionibus orbium coelestium*, astronomy was in crisis, facing multiple problems. Ptolemy's system of astronomy, in which the Earth was at the centre of the universe, had been in use for about 1,500 years, but the inaccuracies were becoming embarrassing and were creating a social pressure for change from several different directions.

The calendar was now obviously wrong, because the equinox had slipped from the twenty-first to the eleventh day of the month, and as this defined the date of Easter and all the other religious festivals it was a serious problem. This wasn't actually due to the physics – it was just that the year wasn't exactly 365 days as had been assumed by the Julian Calendar – but astronomers' efforts to correct the discrepancies were increasing astronomy's complexity far faster than its accuracy. This helped create a desire for change within the scientific community and greater openness for new ways of looking for solutions.

The merchants were unhappy, because Portuguese and Spanish sailors had to use astronomical tables to navigate on their expeditions to the Far East and America, so the tables needed to be accurate, but they weren't.

Philosophers were also demanding change. Whereas in the past they had been happy for mathematics merely to be used to describe the movement of the heavens, leaving the physical truth as a matter for God, the Renaissance Neoplatonists thought that knowledge of mathematics would provide access to the divine mind. This meant that it was important for mathematics to represent the underlying physical truth too, which was something that the insanely complex Ptolemaic universe clearly didn't do.

These multiple crises – in astronomy, philosophy, religion and commerce – created the conditions for a scientific revolution.

Nevertheless, as we'll see in Chapter 8, the ideas took some time to get adopted.

This sense of pressure from multiple directions can be equally effective in encouraging people to wake up to more minor ideas, because people feel much more comfortable if they believe they are part of the majority consensus. You will be much less likely to be ignored as just an isolated voice if, when you call, they think, "I've heard about that somewhere before."

Some companies use this deliberately, employing people to go on web forums to pretend to be "ordinary users" and promote products, ranging from IT hardware to mobile phones and music albums. Some do it very skilfully so it's hard to notice, while others crash around, achieving very little except to irritate other users of the forum.

In a similar vein, in 2006 the Union of Concerned Scientists (UCS) reported that ExxonMobil had provided nearly $16 million in funding since 1998 for 43 advocacy organizations to create uncertainty about the human causes of climate change.[124] This created a highly effective echo chamber of seemingly independent groups.

Alden Meyer, UCS's director of Strategy and Policy, said, "ExxonMobil has manufactured uncertainty about the human causes of global warming just as tobacco companies denied their product caused lung cancer… A modest but effective investment has allowed the oil giant to fuel doubt about global warming to delay government action just as Big Tobacco did for over forty years."

The UCS report revealed that the funding went to an array of organizations, including the well-known George C. Marshall Institute as well as other less widely known groups, with an overlapping collection of individuals serving as staff, board members and scientific advisers. By continually publishing, re-publishing and cross-referencing the works of a small group of climate change contrarians, they cleverly created the appearance of a broad platform of support for their minority views.

Whether or not one approves of their aims, one has to admire the effectiveness of their tactics.

Making them care

In parallel with providing the clear evidence that the status quo is no longer OK, the second element of the unfreezing process is to make your recipient care about it.

At the simplest level this is about focusing your energies where they will do most good: discussing the right topic with the right person at the right time. This seems obvious, but it's surprising how often it's ignored.

For example, cycle campaigners are not all as skilled as the group referred to in Chapter 5. Another group succeeded in persuading a traffic engineer from their city council to meet them at a dangerous junction to discuss how it could be made safer for cyclists. He'd turned up on his bike, so this should have been a good opportunity to get him interested and involved. Unfortunately, however, rather than spending their time showing him things like the dangerous details of the road layout that he could actually do something about, their frustration spilled out in a tirade about the government's inadequate cycling policy.

The engineer was powerless to influence this, so the campaigners' tirade probably made him less likely to feel motivated to help. Worse, they had wasted so much time ranting that they hadn't been able to show him all the dangerous junctions they'd planned to do, and so their opportunity to get their ideas across was largely wasted.

Physics professors suffer a similar problem. They often receive unsolicited manuscripts describing an amateur scientist's "hypothesis" about the nature of the universe. These are usually long and detailed, sometimes using a mathematical notation of the author's own devising. Reading and responding to each one would take hours, if not days, but the chance that the author is another Einstein is infinitesimally small (Einstein was a patent clerk when he published his first three groundbreaking papers). Several physicists have told me that their standard response is just to wait a few months and then reply, quite truthfully, "I can't see anything wrong with it."

Ideas for better mousetraps, suggestions for better ways of doing things at work, unsolicited CVs and book proposals all suffer the same fate. Their creators would have a much better chance if they paid more attention to how to make the recipient feel that the effort involved in reading their work would be worthwhile, rather than assuming that its brilliance would be self-evident.

Picking your topic so that it's relevant to the person you're trying to influence is an important first step, but if they're frozen it will not be enough on its own to make them take action.

We get evidence all the time that something around us isn't working out the way we wanted: the train is late, the weather is horrible or the coffee machine is broken. However, although we notice it and might possibly complain about it, in most cases we don't take it personally, and so we're not motivated to change the way we do things or go out looking for new ideas for how to solve the problem.

Edgar Schein points out that to unfreeze people we need to make them care on a deeper level by inducing either anxiety or guilt, sometimes both, but do it in an environment in which it is safe to care.

If the evidence shows that some goal that is important to us is not being achieved, we feel anxious. For example, if the delayed train means we won't get to an important job interview on time, we start actively looking for ideas for alternative ways to get to our destination. If the evidence makes us feel that we are failing to achieve an ideal, or failing to defend values that are important to us, we feel guilty. This may be guilt about something immediate and tangible like making sure our children have enough to eat (or can wear the right brand-name trainers), or something more remote, like world poverty.

Many campaigners are motivated by a deep sense of outrage that their important values are being violated: for example, the injustice of third-world debt, the lack of care for the natural environment or the mistreatment of children. Whistleblowers may be motivated to take significant risks with their career because of outrage about immoral behaviour that they see happening in their working environment. This feeling of outrage may start as helpless frustration and anger. However, when people realize that there is something they can do to help stop the violation of their values they start feeling guilty if they don't act and it nags away at them until they do.

Providing this sense of agency is a very important part of any campaign, but it's also important in innovation. Inventors are often motivated by noticing something that doesn't work as well as it should, or looks clunky and inelegant: it's a violation of the way things "ought" to be. If they feel helpless to put it right they often become cynical and frustrated, or else put their creativity to work in becoming outspoken critics or creative troublemakers. However, if it's in a field in which they have the skills and opportunity to turn it into a thing of beauty and "rightness", then, just as with the campaigners, it nags away at them until they put it right. This means that if you want to involve a creative person in your idea, often the best way to do this is not to tell them in detail about your proposed solution, but to highlight the inelegance of the current situation or the gaps in your idea, and point out that you need their help because they, and perhaps they alone, can turn it into a thing of beauty.

These feelings of guilt and anxiety can be very powerful, so, for example, making criminals care can reduce crime.

In contrast to conventional criminal justice, which focuses on using punishment and fear to deter repeat offences, "restorative justice" focuses on persuasion, making people care about the consequences of their actions. In restorative justice, the criminal meets face to face with their victim and a facilitator to understand and discuss the impact of their crime. A 2007 review showed that this almost always reduced re-offending, sometimes by as much as 50% in comparison to conventional justice programmes.[125] It also helped victims recover from the crime faster.

It is believed that this works because people who commit crimes often believe, or convince themselves, that they are not acting immorally.

Restorative justice engages them in discussion about whether it really is wrong, and then helps them redefine themselves as not the kind of people who would do immoral things. It works best when it's emotionally powerful, which is probably why it is most effective with violent offences against people (rather than property crime), and with offenders who have enough empathy to identify with their victims. It can also be very effective with young people who have committed their first offence.

This needs a skilled facilitator; restorative justice is not a simple "box ticking" exercise.

The effect of making people care on a deep and emotional level is so powerful that even mediocre ideas can get adopted.

In the UK, the growing awareness of our personal contribution to climate change is making increasing numbers of people feel guilty about flying and hence start looking for ideas for solutions. Some decide to travel by train instead of taking short-haul flights, but others take up the simpler offer of "guilt-free flying" and buy carbon offsets. Even though there is serious debate about whether it really does any good in reducing climate change, and some of the less reputable offsetting companies are virtually scams, sales in the unregulated "voluntary offset market" increased from three million to fifty million tonnes between 2004 and 2006, and by early 2007 there were at least thirty different schemes.[126] Offsetting is clearly tapping into a deeply rooted need to reduce a growing sense of guilt, whether or not it is really a good idea.

Positive emotions, like fun, love, or spotting an opportunity, do also help motivate people, but it's important to realize that they are much less powerful than guilt and anxiety, and so often won't be enough on their own. This is why people who feel threatened by your idea will be much more voluble and energetic than the people who like it. It also means that even if people say they love your idea, it's most unwise to assume that they will actually do anything to help you. It's easy to bask in the glow of satisfaction, but more effective if you have the courage to ask, "Why do you like it?", and then tap into their deeper motivations. For example, you might sense an anxiety that if you took your product idea to a competitor, they might then get ahead.

If you are trying to interest a company in your innovation, the best prospects are often not with the obvious market leader, but with the second-ranking company, one that is feeling threatened, anxious, or maybe guilty in some way, so wants new ideas. The market leader will often be complacent and interested in maintaining the status quo, and may well waste your time by expressing interest and having long drawn out discussions, but never signing a deal.

People vary

Making people care needs skill and flexibility, because people vary a lot in what they care about and what motivates them. If you make people care too much, they will be paralyzed by guilt and anxiety. If you don't make them care enough, nothing will happen.

Consider what happens when a skilled car salesman tries to make a sale. The buyer has probably already had some sort of evidence that has made him less satisfied with his current car. Maybe it is becoming unreliable, is starting to feel like an embarrassing gas-guzzler, or looks feeble in comparison to the next-door neighbour's high-performance sports car.

The salesman will try to find out what the buyer is looking for in order to understand what goals or ideals are not being met. He will then try to focus on this and exploit it by subtly making the buyer feel guilty or anxious unless he buys the car. For example, he might empathize about the horrific cost of repairs, talk about all the environmental improvements in the new model, or enthuse about its power, performance and pulling power with the girls.

He will help his chances of making a sale if he can pick the right issue to focus on and increase the buyer's level of guilt and anxiety about it, but offer the purchase of a new car as the way to resolve it.

It is, of course, very important to pick the right issue to focus on, because people vary a lot in how they are motivated by their underlying beliefs and values. The brand-development expert Pat Dade studies this and has been monitoring trends in the UK and elsewhere for 30 years.[127] His work suggests that at present about 44% of people in the UK are "outer driven", or concerned about appearance, status and what other people think about them, while 35% are "inner driven", or more likely to be idealists and open to new ideas for the future, and 21% are driven by a need for security and belonging.

It is therefore very important to realize that what feels natural and motivating to you may not engage others. Many campaigners and innovators are inner driven; for example, in the early days of Greenpeace about 80% of staff were inner driven – very different from the wider UK population.

If you are inner driven and trying to spread the idea of a low-carbon lifestyle, your idealism may mean that you personally feel good about giving up your car, getting on your bicycle and campaigning for better public transport; however, you'll struggle to engage people in the other groups. People who are outer driven will be much more likely to be interested in the idea of putting a visible status symbol like solar panels or wind turbines on their house, or exchanging their car for the high-tech hybrid that they see celebrities driving. People who are security driven will be more likely to be motivated by the savings, comfort and security they'll get from improving the level of insulation in their home or installing a wood-burning stove. These are all effective ways to move to a low-carbon lifestyle, but tap into very different motivations.

If you are serious about getting your ideas adopted, you'll need to adapt your message to your audience so you make them care.

Providing the safety to care

Providing safety is perhaps the most valuable and most neglected element of the unfreezing process, because it provides a way to channel the energy created by making people care. Clear evidence makes us realize that the status quo isn't OK, while our feelings of guilt or anxiety make us care about it. However, without a sense of safety we will remain frozen, adopting all sorts of defence mechanisms to protect ourselves from the painful feelings rather than looking calmly and rationally at the merits of the idea in front of us.

Psychological "safety" gives us the sense of security that allows us to deal with these defences, to care about difficult and important issues and use our creativity to tackle them.

It deflates resistance, rather than trying to overpower it.

A supportive environment

The simplest way to create a sense of safety is to provide a supportive environment and help people feel that other people like them are tackling the same issues successfully. This sense of togetherness is a very powerful motivator, and is part of the secret of success of buzzy creative companies or support groups like Alcoholics Anonymous.

When I am working with people who are facing a daunting challenge, I find that quite often all that is necessary is to help them realize that their nervousness about doing something new is quite normal and that in reality they are perfectly competent to handle it. As they get to grips with the problem and realize that this is indeed true, they stop needing the moral support and encouragement, and so take full responsibility themselves.

Enthusiastic, idealistic young people working in the voluntary sector are particularly vulnerable to working so hard that they drive themselves to exhaustion and burn-out. The psychotherapist Rosemary Randall points out that one of the reasons for this is that they try to compensate for the rest of the world's lack of interest in the problems they see by internalizing a sense of guilt.[128] It's impossible ever to do enough to solve these problems, so they drive themselves to the point of collapse.

With increasing maturity or support, campaigners realize that they don't need to solve all the world's problems, so they become much better at focusing their efforts in an area in which they feel they can make a difference. As one philanthropist said to me, "You can't do everything. You just have to focus and feel good about what you *can* do."

By meeting and working with others you realize that you are not alone: other people are trying to address the problems you can't deal with. This lets you lay aside your sense of guilt about them, regain your energy and enthusiasm and feel the pleasure of achievement that comes from making progress in the area you've chosen to focus on.

We all face stresses in our work, but if the environment isn't supportive, we will find other ways to deal with the anxiety of the job. People working in emotionally stressful jobs (such as assessing evidence of torture submitted in support of applications for asylum, or closing down child pornography websites) very often use *M*A*S*H*-style black humour. To an outsider it may seem grossly inappropriate, but it's an important mechanism to help caring staff cope.

Larry Hirschhorn, the eminent American consultant on the psychodynamics of organizations, points out that anxiety reduction is also one of the reasons that organizations become bureaucratic.[129] If you work in a bank, it's much easier to fall back on the bank's rules and processes for assessing lending applications, rather than make your own judgement about whether someone is in need of money, or will default on a loan.

This can have an impact on the ways in which people adopt ideas. For example, some research I did once amongst engineers and scientists showed that people in organizations that they described as "hierarchical and bureaucratic" were most likely to deal with the anxiety of the job by getting out of the office. No one mentioned talking to their peers. In total contrast, people working in an organization that they described as having "high autonomy and networking" were most likely to deal with the anxieties of the job by talking to their peers. No one mentioned finding that getting out of the office helped.

This means that if you are trying to get people to adopt ideas in an organization, it's worth thinking about what will work best in that environment. People in bureaucratic organizations will definitely find it easier to be relaxed and receptive if they are out of the office. They love "away days". People in more "organic" organizations may find it more useful to hold the meeting in their office, so they can more easily discuss the idea with their peers.

Clear first steps

It also helps unfreeze people if you can make the scale of the problems feel manageable, so, for example, rather than telling someone that their performance is "all wrong", pick one aspect and get them to focus on sorting that out first. Similarly, successful campaigns may apply pressure to politicians, but they also provide a way out. As the chief executive of one influential NGO put it, "a small hole we can squirt them through".

If you are trying to get your family to agree that you need to do a total makeover on your house, they may well have accepted that something needs to be done and like the general idea of how it could be improved. However, they may still put off doing anything about it, because they feel very daunted by the disruption that it will all involve.

You can often unlock this if you can suggest a simple and clear first step along the road, such as "Why don't we start by sorting out the children's bedrooms?"

The pleasure and satisfaction people get from the results will help encourage them to carry on. If you have been careful to think ahead, each step will steadily build towards your vision. It is, however, important to be flexible, because the idea will probably steadily improve with each step you take, just as the view becomes better as you climb a hill.

Sometimes we miss very simple opportunities to unfreeze people by giving them a clear sense of the next steps. For example, in one recent case I was involved in, an engineer was feeling rather frustrated by marketing colleagues who were refusing to provide the input he needed and stalling his project. Trying to gee them up, he said, "If you don't make your minds up about what you want, we won't be able to get started."

Unfortunately, this did very little to unfreeze the marketing people: they were busy, so it was quite attractive to think that engineering would have to sit around while they decided what the customers might want. The rather negative language also helped reinforce their prejudice that engineering didn't do a lot.

It would have been much more likely to have delivered results if the engineer had worded it in a much more energetic and forward looking way; for example, "I need you to give me at least a gut feel for what you want by the end of the month, so we can launch at next year's trade fair."

The specific, achievable actions and timescales would have helped unfreeze them while conveying a sense of openness to ideas, urgency and progress.

Dealing with defences

As we saw earlier, we all use a variety of defence mechanisms to protect ourselves from painful emotions. This is natural and helpful, helping us reduce the pain of bereavement until we're strong enough to face it, or helping us deal with the anxieties of a stressful job. However, the feelings can also paralyze us, or force us into bizarre behaviour.

For example, if you are working in the healthcare system, it is naturally very distressing to dwell too much on all the human suffering you deal with on the wards, so to protect yourself you might take a relentlessly positive view, denying the pain and suffering, or alternatively regress into just thinking about bed occupancy rates and waiting lists.

A sad and extreme example of this is Barbara Salisbury, a senior ward sister in a UK hospital who was sentenced to five years in 2004 for attempting to murder two elderly patients under her care. It became clear during the trial that she had been motivated by an excessive desire to free up beds at a hospital which was in the throes of a bed-blocking crisis.[130] This was a high profile problem at the time, in which elderly patients had to be kept in hospital for months longer than was clinically necessary, because there were no beds available for them in care homes. It is important to realize that Salisbury was no monster. She had been a nurse for nearly thirty years and was well regarded by managers as efficient, although her brisk manner made her somewhat unpopular with other nurses.

Many of the techniques for dealing with defences come from counselling and therapy, where people's defences have become pathological and damaging. The key principle is that the therapist uses a combination of listening and carefully focused interventions to help the patient find their own solution; therapists know that solutions imposed from outside will be ignored. Although in most non-clinical situations people's defences aren't nearly so strong or so damaging, I find that these ideas are very useful in unlocking resistance to ideas, giving people the safety to relax and deal openly and creatively with the challenges facing them.

For example, Rosemary Randall, who as well as being a psychotherapist is also the director of the Cambridge-based group Cambridge Carbon Footprint, was working through a questionnaire with a client to work out his carbon footprint, when suddenly the client stopped her and said, "I think you're all very admirable, but it won't work because everyone is selfish."

He was a smart guy, and had realized that the result of the questionnaire was that he was going to be made to feel that various things that he liked doing were "bad" and selfish. To defend himself against this feeling, he stopped the interview, but in a typical defence reaction, blamed his selfish feelings on others rather than taking ownership of them himself (psychotherapists refer to this process as "projection").

Rosemary initially tried pointing out that self-interest could also be useful for persuading people to reduce their carbon emissions, but this logical argument didn't address the source of the resistance. Rosemary then changed tack, and started asking him about himself. When it became apparent that he was a social worker, Rosemary pointed out that this wasn't a selfish profile; he must be working long hours for low pay, so maybe there were other people who were the same? People could be complex mixtures of emotions. This got through, and the man switched again and acknowledged that he too could be both selfish and altruistic. He completed the questionnaire, and went off with a low-energy light bulb, full of enthusiasm to reduce his carbon impact.

By listening to him and creating a safe place to discuss his feelings and fears about the impact of climate change on his lifestyle, Rosemary very neatly deflated his resistance to the idea of reducing his carbon footprint.

Reducing the fear of risk

One of the most common objections to a new idea is that it's too risky.

Although inevitably there will be some truth in this, because new ideas always have imperfections and very seldom work out quite like the inventor expects, this common apparent paranoia about risk is very frustrating.

One of the reasons for it is that different people have different perceptions about risk. For some people, like the Careful Conservators we saw in Chapter 2, it's very important to have everything under control and well organized, so they try to reduce risk and uncertainty. For other people, particularly some of the personality types that are most likely to be highly creative, risk and uncertainty feel energizing and exciting.

To some extent our preference for risk may be caused by our brain chemistry. Spanish researchers showed that bullfighters often have unusually low levels of an enzyme called monoamine oxidase in their blood.[131] In contrast, people who suffer from panic attacks because of something as simple as a visit to a shopping centre sometimes have unusually high levels of the enzyme. Drugs do exist to reduce the enzyme levels, called monoamine oxidase inhibitors, which are also sometimes used as a last resort treatment for depression. Unfortunately, however, they are not suitable for use on risk-averse recipients of your idea; they are complicated and powerful drugs, which can have lethal side effects![132]

This difference in perception about the level of risk that feels comfortable and energizing can often get us into trouble. If we're the Creative Maverick personality type we often try to energize people by emphasizing how new and different our idea is. However, for many personality types, we'd do a lot better to make it sound only marginally different from the conventional way of doing it, while of course emphasizing the idea's benefits.

To those of us who are Creative Mavericks this feels as if it makes the idea boring, but nevertheless it works.

As we saw earlier, we are more influenced by the views of our peers than we might like to think. This effect can be very useful for reducing the fear of risk of your ideas, so, for example, some smart companies that are trying to sell innovative products to other businesses start by trying to make a good impression on relevant opinion leaders. This means that when potential customers start asking around to reassure themselves about the risk of purchasing, there's a better chance they'll hear something favourable.

It will help your idea take off if you can find safe ways for people to try it out, without risking disaster or humiliation if it goes wrong. This is particularly important if the recipient is in an environment that, rightly or wrongly, penalizes mistakes and failures.

Engineers will make a prototype to test a design and iron out mistakes before commissioning expensive injection moulding tooling for plastic components. Supermarkets will test market a new product in one or two stores before going national with it. Wise organizations pilot new processes and ideas to make sure they work, always aiming to take the opportunity to learn and refine the innovation. Foolish ones all too often feel that any changes would count as a failure, so blithely roll out the pilot nationally, warts and all.

For example, in 2004, UK family doctors were given a target to see patients within 24 hours. It seemed like an obvious good idea at the time (at least to its initiators high up in the Department of Health), and so was rolled out across the UK. Too late it became apparent that doctors were meeting the target by refusing to let patients forward-book appointments, even if they wanted to, while patients had to spend days trying to get an appointment. At the 2005 election, in a storm of outrage and media coverage, Tony Blair had to admit that the situation was absurd and that "something should be done about it".

The consequences of making a mistake in your idea depend on what it is. Use the wrong font in your new design of cat-food packaging and you may feel annoyed and get into trouble, but the wider world may not even notice. Make a mistake when designing an ejector seat in a fighter jet and someone may die.

This means that sometimes the best way to get new ideas adopted is to find an application in a "safe" field, where failure won't be disastrous. Although initially these areas may seem second best, often they turn out to be gold mines.

In the late 1990s two small UK companies were developing superficially similar devices for generating intense and very short pulses of bright light. It had been recognized for some time that this technology had a number of interesting biomedical applications, so, for example, it could "see" developing melanomas (skin cancer) before they were visible to the naked eye.

For one of the companies, this was the obvious application. They told me later, "We felt confident that if we could develop a device that could see early-stage skin cancers, the world would beat a path to our door."

However, they found it much more difficult to get the idea accepted than they had expected. In part it was because medical diagnostics is a highly regulated area, but they also found surprising resistance from surgeons. They told me that slowly they realized that this was because surgeons in the USA remove 100 moles for every one that is cancerous, so the last thing they want is a device that will reduce their business by 99%. For all their good intentions, seven years later, the company is still struggling to make money out of the idea.

The other company, Energist-International, started by focusing on a rather less glamorous area: hair removal.[133] Although this had been known as a "side effect" of using intense pulsed light sources since the 1970s, a local laser physicist got interested in the idea when he accidentally shot himself with the light beam and found that the hair never grew back. Some time later a plastic surgeon was searching for a method to remove hair from a skin graft. This got the company thinking and they quickly realized that as there was a rapidly increasing $2.5 billion global market for hair removal, the market for a cost-effective device that removed hair painlessly and virtually permanently should be very interesting. As they told me, "We realized that the money is in the mass market, not clinical applications."

They were not alone in realizing this and had competitors, but they did well and tripled in size between 2001 and 2006, supplying hundreds of systems to clinics in Japan, Australia and the USA. By 2007 they calculated that someone was being treated with one of their systems once every 12 seconds.

Energist-International did well by focusing on the side effect, rather than the obvious clinical application, but starting in a "safe" area can also be a way to build experience in preparation for accessing the more difficult market later.

In 1970 the Japanese firm Toray decided to invest 1.5 billion yen (equivalent to approximately $150 million today) in a manufacturing plant for a recently invented material, carbon fibre.[134] The plant could produce five times more than the world needed at the time, but they thought it was worth the risk; they had the vision to see that composite materials would be very important replacements for steel and aluminium alloys in applications where strength and weight were important. The aviation industry was the obvious example.

Nevertheless, although Toray were prepared to take the risk, they struggled to persuade the aviation industry to accept it. In 1972 they took an alternative tack, when an American golf pro won a Japanese tournament using a carbon fibre club. This was a much safer market for an innovative new material than aerospace, so Toray developed a range of different fibres to allow ever-better, stiffer clubs and the market began to grow rapidly. It was only after the oil crises of the 1980s that the aircraft market became important, at which time Toray also developed a rather different range of stronger fibres to suit its needs. Today Toray are the world's most successful carbon fibre producer, with 34% of the global market.[135]

Are they frozen, or is the idea rubbish?

When a radical idea is being resisted, it can be hard to tell at the time whether this is a reasonable response to an unreasonable idea, or an indication that your opponent is frozen.

Telepathy is an interesting example. A poll by the US National Science Foundation (NSF) in 2001 showed that 60% of the US population agreed with the statement that "some people possess psychic powers or ESP".

As Dr Dean Radin, laboratory director for the Institute of Noetic Sciences in Petaluma, California, points out in his fascinating book *The Conscious Universe*, the cumulative scientific evidence that telepathy is a real effect is now as strong as the evidence that aspirin reduces the risk of heart attacks.[136] The evidence is particularly strong when it is done under so-called "ganzfeld" conditions. These minimize the external distractions for the "recipient" by sitting them in a comfortable chair in a dimly lit room with half ping-pong balls over their eyes and lightly hissing headphones on their ears. This makes it very easy to go into an almost trance-like state, which seems to make it easier to pick up the picture that the "sender" is trying to get you to see from another room. Surprisingly, although the design of the experiments means that one would only expect to be able to guess correctly 25% of the time, on average people are right 34% of the time.

These results have been widely replicated, and are very intriguing. But greatly to the frustration of parapsychology's supporters, the results are ignored by most mainstream scientists: less than 2% of mainstream psychology departments have any faculty working on it at all.[137]

Logically, the evidence for ganzfeld telepathy should be very convincing because it's based on thousands of experimental sessions, done in accordance with experimental protocols that were developed and agreed with the sceptics. However, accepting the evidence would mean overturning mental models that are deeply embedded (at least in the scientific community in the West). These take for granted that we are all isolated individuals, that our consciousness is located inside our heads, and that we can only use the known physical senses to communicate.

At present the experimental results on ganzfeld telepathy are of no professional interest at all to most people in the scientific community, except for a few scientists in the newly emerging field of consciousness studies and some open minded physicists interested in the implications of "quantum entanglement".[138] This is a mind-boggling area of physics in which fundamental particles such as photons can influence each other at a distance, purely because they were once together and their properties are now entangled. Nevertheless, entangling individual photons is very different from entangling minds.

It is perhaps significant that although there's a trickle of research carried out by relatively poorly resourced independent scientists and labs, the most prominent organizations that have been involved in telepathy research to date are the CIA and Sony. In both cases their work was initially secret, which no doubt helped give people the psychological safety to give it a go. In each case, there were other factors that helped the organization unfreeze enough to start their exploration.

For the CIA it was fear of a threat: always a powerful motivator. From 1972 to 1988 the CIA sponsored research at Stanford Research Institute and subsequently the Science Applications International Corporation (SAIC) in Menlo Park, California, to determine whether such phenomena as remote viewing "might have any utility for intelligence collection". The programme was mostly devoted to threat assessment, and after it was declassified in 1995 the programme's former director, Dr H. E. Puthoff, commented that it produced "some brilliant successes, many total failures".[139] He concluded by saying, "Despite the ambiguities inherent in the type of exploration covered in these programs, the integrated results appear to provide unequivocal evidence of a human capacity to access events remote in space and time, however falteringly, by some cognitive process not yet understood."

The concept of some sort of connection between individuals is much less alien to most people in Japan than it is in the West, so it is perhaps unsurprising that the first major commercial company to explore parapsychology was Japanese.

In 1990 Sony set up its parapsychology lab, ESPER (Extrasensory Perception and Excitation Research). This was led by Yoichiro Sako, a computer scientist from their multimedia labs who had got interested in parapsychology. With the help of Sony's co-founder Masaru Ibuka he got approval for his proposal "to investigate the scientific evidence supporting the idea of Qi". This is a biological "life force" accepted by many eastern belief systems. The lab explored the nature of Qi, but also many aspects of remote viewing and telepathy. Although initially its existence was kept secret, in 1995 Sony went public, presenting the ESPER lab as a demonstration of Sony's role in developing exciting possible future technologies. The Japanese media became very excited and public opinion was largely positive. However, much of the resistance came from within Sony itself, so it was perhaps unsurprising that when Masaru Ibuka died in 1997, the lab was closed within six months.

Sony's spokesman, Masanobu Sakaguchi, explained in the *South China Morning Post* in July 1998, "We found out experimentally that yes, ESP exists, but that any practical application of this knowledge is not likely in the foreseeable future."

As a commercial organization this was probably a wise decision. Although they found that Qi Gong practitioners could pretty reliably use their hands to detect Qi, they still had no idea how to detect, use or store Qi with a machine. It was therefore hard to see how an organization like Sony could make money out of it.

Is the resistance to parapsychology because the sceptics are frozen, or because the idea's rubbish? It's always hard to tell, but there are two classic signs that suggest that this is a real phenomenon, battling against frozen sceptics.

Firstly, the evidence: it isn't definitive, but it never is in early stage ideas. As usual, there is also a lot of rubbish around from self-proclaimed "paranormal investigators", TV magicians and cranks. However, it's important not to let this overshadow the real research from experiments that are designed with much tighter experimental controls than are applied in other, less controversial, areas of social science or psychology. Nevertheless, the underlying mechanism may well not be quite what its proponents expect.

The second warning sign that people are frozen is the behaviour of the sceptics, some of whom are certainly frozen about it. The biologist Rupert Sheldrake described how biologist and telepathy-sceptic Lewis Wolpert deliberately turned his back on Sheldrake's presentation so he could continue to say that he hadn't seen any evidence in support of telepathy.[140] When people take trouble to avoid hearing about an idea, it is a good sign that they are frozen, letting their fear of the disruption from the idea overwhelm their normal rational curiosity about a potentially important phenomenon. As one would expect, it is those with more motivation or more accommodating mental models and personality that have been pioneering the exploration.

It may well take a long time before there has been sufficiently broad progress and a sufficiently long period of scientific insecurity for scientists to accept something with such transformational impact.

The history of science suggests that scientists will only accept telepathy when it offers answers to a crisis in "normal science", when society is demanding answers or when it becomes apparent that the idea doesn't actually disagree too much with established mental models after all.

If the idea actually starts to become useful and predictable, it's often surprising how readily people will adopt it and start using it, just so long as they can ignore the fact that the scientists can't really explain it. Anaesthetists have told me that no one really understands how anaesthetics work. Engineers have used experimentally derived formulas to calculate the rate at which water will flow down a pipe for over a hundred years, even though physicists have only very recently been able to model what is going on.[141] Even a strange and totally unexplained phenomenon like dowsing, also known as water divining, is used quietly and quite widely by water boards and electricity companies to check for buried pipes and cables, or identify places to drill for water.[142]

As with previous outrageous ideas like the heliocentric solar system or continental drift, telepathy's supporters will have to persist, quietly building up evidence, finding ways to connect it with things people care about and then finding ways for them to explore it in safety.

If they are lucky, after many years of frustration and ridicule, quite suddenly, everyone will get interested.

Interested

"Tell me about it"

In the third stage, people are at last interested in hearing about your idea. They are aware of it and, one way or another, are no longer blind to it, no longer frozen by their problems. They are looking for ideas.

So how do you get them hooked?

An important principle is that you can't force someone to adopt an idea, you have to entice them. Somehow, without losing the inspiring vision, you have to let people contribute to the idea and help build it, so that in some way it becomes their idea too.

There are many different ways of doing this depending on the situation you are in. The first part of this chapter focuses on how to use speeches, presentations, questions, demonstrations, stories and images to inspire people and draw them in. How do you excite people about ideas that may well still be unproven, ambiguous and partially intuitive?

The final part of the chapter looks at how to deal with the response you get, because unfortunately people won't necessarily like your idea when they hear about it. You may not realize this initially, because if it doesn't affect them personally they may well keep quiet about their views, only asking the occasional difficult question, but becoming voluble critics when they start to worry that it may actually happen. This can be very frustrating, but as we will see, it is often much more productive to focus on building up your support rather than get distracted into waging war on your opponents.

Inspiring vision

Once people have been released from the frozen grip of their feelings and fears, it is your inspiring vision that will attract their interest. However, vision comes in several different forms.

The classic example and the one that many people think of when you talk about vision is exemplified by Martin Luther King's superb speech in 1963 to over 200,000 civil rights supporters during the March on Washington for Jobs and Freedom.[143]

As we might expect from the last chapter, he started by reminding his audience of the problem facing them, and why they were there.

> But one hundred years later, the Negro still is not free. One hundred years later, the life of the Negro is still sadly crippled by the manacles of segregation and the chains of discrimination. One hundred years later, the Negro lives on a lonely island of poverty in the midst of a vast ocean of material prosperity. One hundred years later, the Negro is still languished in the corners of American society and finds himself an exile in his own land. And so we've come here today to dramatize a shameful condition.

Ten minutes later came the second half of the speech, with his famous description of his dream: "I have a dream that one day this nation will rise up and live out the true meaning of its creed: 'We hold these truths to be self-evident, that all men are created equal.' I have a dream…"

The rhythm and power of his 20-minute speech was so strong that it became the defining moment in the American Civil Rights Movement.

Similarly, in 1940, Sir Winston Churchill faced a disastrous situation. Three hundred and fifty thousand British troops had retreated from Dunkirk a few weeks earlier. Holland, Luxembourg, Belgium and then France had surrendered to the Germans. Britain stood alone facing Hitler's seemingly unstoppable armies.

Churchill needed Parliament to face up to the seriousness of the situation, but without letting it fall victim to recriminations and a perfectly reasonable sense of helplessness. In a landmark speech, he reviewed the dire situation at length, finishing by saying, "Let us therefore brace ourselves to our duties and so bear ourselves that, if the British Empire and its Commonwealth last for a thousand years, men will still say, 'This was their finest hour.'"[144]

Both King and Churchill used the power of their visions and rhetoric to envisage an inspiring future state and contrast it with the dire current situation. Few of us have the power of rhetoric of either man. Fewer still are in such a position of leadership and influence in such a difficult situation. Nevertheless, our visionary ideas can inspire others if we give them a chance.

Natural enthusiasm and exciting ideas

For many creative people, some of their greatest assets are their natural enthusiasm and exciting ideas. Even the Careful Conservator types we saw in Chapter 2 say that these are things that make them more likely to adopt an idea. However, all too often I see people who have an interesting idea, possibly a great idea, but in order to try to reduce the resistance to it they downplay its promise, downplay the vision. Unfortunately this doesn't do anything to reduce the recipient's anxiety about the risks and effort involved in taking the idea on board, but just reduces their motivation to consider it.

It is much more effective to be strong and confident about the vision, but realistic and open about the risks and effort that will be involved in getting there.

For example, Tony Hooley is a serial entrepreneur, and the inventor of the digital surround-sound projector. This allows true surround-sound from a single flat-panel speaker, getting away from the tangled mess of wires that would otherwise be needed to connect up five separate speakers and get cinema quality surround-sound.

He first came up with the idea of making a digital loudspeaker in 1994. It seemed to him that normal loudspeakers were based on a design that was fundamentally unchanged for a hundred years, so he thought, "Surely there has to be a better way of doing it."

As an electronics engineer, he also realized that digital processing was getting cheaper and cheaper, so that almost any amount of processing power he could put together would effectively be free in five years' time. This started him thinking about what he could do with it to make a better speaker. Four years later he had a company, 1 Ltd,[145] with two employees; a year later there were about nine.

Funding the company was a continual struggle: it didn't really make any money for the first ten years. However, Tony Hooley is naturally enthusiastic, and this comes across whenever he speaks, so he became very successful at exciting private investors. One of the largest rooms in their rabbit warren of offices is the demo room, designed to give people an awesome audio experience. Not only can they generate surround sound from a single speaker box, but they can project sound so precisely that two people sitting next to each other can be made to hear completely different things. He says:

> The AGM (Annual General Meeting) was always three minutes of
> formalities, then half an hour of all the exciting things we'd been doing, and
> then some demos, and we'd have investors going away saying "That was
> fantastic, that was the best AGM I've ever been to." The investor network
> has grown enormously because they've been enthused, and have then enthused
> their moneyed friends.

In 2003 the technology was licensed to Yamaha, and in January 2005 the Yamaha Digital Sound Projector was awarded "Best in Show" at the Consumer Electronics Show in Las Vegas, the ultimate accolade of the industry.

Demonstrations are very useful for exciting people about ideas, but part of the art is to excite people about the future potential, rather than suggesting that what they are seeing is the final product. Not only does this let you be more creative, but it also lets you get feedback and hence improve the idea.

The automotive industry shows off its creativity and ideas by demonstrating "concept cars" at trade shows. Many of these are never going to be put into production, but are ways of testing reactions to radical concepts, which are used to inform the design process for future models of much more conventional cars.

Visionary questions

You can't command someone to adopt your ideas. You have to inspire them, engage them or entice them into adopting it. This means that in some situations, it will be much more effective to define inspiring questions or give people exciting options to choose from, rather than trying to impose a concrete idea for a solution.

One person who does this very well is Alison Richard, Vice-Chancellor of Cambridge University. This is an institution that has been in existence since

1209, which is plenty of time to have built up lots of traditions and resistance to change. Universities are never easy to lead, because, as she says, academics don't join universities in order to be led. She therefore puts a lot of emphasis on bringing people together to ask questions and explore issues collaboratively. She once told me, "I see vision as getting the right people thinking hard about the right questions."

Encouraging this sort of questioning, collaborative dialogue can be one of the most productive ways of getting people to adopt ideas, particularly when we are trying to influence people over whom we have no formal authority or when working with people who refuse to accept what authority we do have.

Stimulating people to search for their own solution in this way can take a little longer than trying to engage them in your idea, but it can also result in a better, more robust result, because if people are searching for their own solutions, they will automatically notice and pick up the information and ideas that fit with their mental models.

Impossible, but not too impossible

Visions engage if they are attractive and challenging, but they will be ignored if they seem ridiculous, just as the European astronomers ignored sunspots for at least 1,600 years longer than the Chinese.

Leonardo da Vinci's 1483 design for a helicopter was only thought of as a toy, not least because there was no practical power source available for a full-sized flying machine. However, four centuries later his sketch inspired Igor Sikorsky, a Ukrainian American who designed the first truly practical helicopter, which went into production in the early years of the Second World War.

If you have a visionary goal that many people will think impossible or unattractive, you can also follow the example of the pioneers of the European Union. They defined their vision as "ever closer union".

This was simple and engaging, but disguised very significant differences of opinion between the countries about how far and how fast they wanted to go towards union. For example, the French civil servant Jean Monnet, widely regarded as the architect of the European Union, had the creation of a federal Europe as an ultimate goal. They prudently approached this step by step, starting with six countries and the creation of the boringly named "European Coal and Steel Community". By 2007 the European Union had 27 member countries, 13 of which had the euro as their sole currency, an elected parliament and law making powers. It is not yet a federal Europe, but is certainly well down the path to ever closer union.

Effective presentations

As creative people, we often have ideas and visions for the future that feel overwhelmingly brilliant, but we can't get other people to recognise them.

It's never easy explaining ideas, because they are often uncertain and still partially intuitive, so we ourselves may have difficulty articulating them. We also need to walk the tightrope so that we are clear, inspiring and visionary, but at the same time we are genuinely involving others in helping build the idea. If we have a genuinely good idea and can do all these things, which is no mean feat, we will find that people start to adopt our idea and make it their own.

Although mass communication may be important later, at this early stage much of the work of persuasion will be done face to face. This is a much more effective way of involving people and getting embryonic ideas across than more impersonal ways such as writing memos, emails and websites, or (sadly, as an author) even writing books.

For many budding entrepreneurs their most stressful experience is giving an "elevator pitch" to a group of potential investors. Typically they have just ten minutes to get their audiences interested. If successful they can raise several hundred thousand pounds to finance their businesses and acquire themselves some "business angels"; successful entrepreneurs who will provide not only financial backing, but also the even more important advice and contacts. If they fail they have to continue the soul destroying process of trying to raise the funding they need to make their ideas real.

The terror of this experience is the basis for the successful BBC TV programme *Dragon's Den*, in which would-be entrepreneurs face humiliation pitching their business ideas to five notoriously aggressive and sceptical multi-millionaires. If successful they can win up to £150,000 in investment from the "dragons". However, even if unsuccessful they have had the opportunity to explain their idea on primetime TV to an audience of over 3.5 million, which can often be worth much more.

One of the contestants who got a roasting was Rachel Lowe. She was a 29-year-old taxi driver and mother of two when she invented the board game Destinations in 2002. She was so excited about the potential that she went back to college to study business, and got herself a business loan and local sponsorship to produce the game. Two years later she appeared on *Dragon's Den*. She says that she learned some useful lessons from her roasting, but that it turned out to be a blessing in disguise: by chance, her episode was screened in early 2005, when she was exhibiting at a toy fair.

She says, "Everyone kept coming by the stand, and customers were saying, 'You proved them wrong, you go, girl.' The dragons did me a favour; without the slating I wouldn't have got the public and trade support."[146]

Luck plays an important role for most entrepreneurs, but Rachel Lowe's story also demonstrates the need to keep up your morale even through horrible experiences.

People often expect reality to be like the TV programme, but it is important to remember that *Dragon's Den* is entertainment, so candidates are often selected to be quirky and are set up to be humiliated. As Hugh Parnell, former director of one of the UK's top business angel networks says, "*Dragon's Den* doesn't show the bits that matter – it's just about humiliation and easy laughs."[147]

Real life is very different, so although you can expect to be asked probing questions, they will be from people who are genuinely interested in trying to spot winners.

If you are trying to pitch your ideas for real, rather than for entertainment, how should you do it? Clearly your approach will be somewhat different depending on whether you are pitching a business idea to potential investors, explaining your idea to your boss over the coffee machine or trying to persuade your friends to try drinking in a new bar. Nevertheless, there are five key universal principles to remember when pitching ideas. I refer to these as Who, Why, What, Hook and How.

Who, Why, What, Hook and How

1 Who (are you?)

People buy ideas from people, so it's vitally important to make sure that they feel they can believe and trust you. Does your past experience suggest that you are likely to be right? Do you understand what the market needs? Do you have the self-awareness to know what you don't know? Who else supports you? Do you seem enthusiastic and yet realistic?

Experienced people know that it takes a lot of work to make a bright idea real, so they look for the passion and drive that will enable you to keep going, just so long as this doesn't cross the borderline into naive credulity.

One study of how chief executives make decisions showed that while most people base them on the information that's most accessible, CEOs put much more emphasis on digging out high-quality sources of information that they can trust.[148] Conveying this impression of trustworthiness (and making sure you don't lose it) is probably the most important thing you can do to get your ideas adopted.

2 Why (is this a good idea?)

Without an apparent benefit, there's nothing to motivate someone to go to the effort of exploring your idea.

Why does the world want this? What is the evidence that you are right? All too often, Creative Mavericks and Visionary Leaders blow their chances by forgetting to explain the benefits and rationale for the idea, because to them it seems so blindingly obvious. If you are talking to a Careful Conservator or Innovative Trouble-Shooter personality type, it's also important to remember that it's experience, data and facts that make them feel comfortable, so include lots.

In some commercial situations a "good idea" is one that competitors can't copy (perhaps because of a patent or your unique specialist know-how). In other situations, good ideas are ones that will spread virally.

In 2004, while the music industry complained about piracy and copyright theft, the four teenagers of the Sheffield-based band Arctic Monkeys were giving away demo discs, letting fans copy and share them on the Internet. Although they themselves were total Internet novices (fans put them on MySpace before they even knew what it was), this built up a huge fan base which took them to the top of the UK charts before their first single was even released.

3 What (is the big idea?)

It is your inspiring vision that will excite people and help move them from passivity into action. Although the detail of your idea may be quite complex, you need to be able to explain your vision in just a few sentences, and it's a useful exercise to try to cut this down to just nine words. This means that when you bump into the chief executive in the lift, you can explain the essence of your idea and why it's special before she gets out at the next floor. For example, "It's a tool-free blade changing system for jigsaws," "It's the first radio station for the Romany community," or "It's a book about getting your ideas adopted."

Ideally this will make them interested enough to ask for more detail.

As we'll see later in this chapter, illustrations and stories are also very useful to help make intuitive ideas graspable and memorable.

4 Hook (to their interests)

As we saw in the last chapter, people will only be motivated to explore an idea if it connects with their interests and seems beneficial. If you are pitching to investors, you need to have done your figures so you can talk about the financial return. On the other hand, if you are talking to Formula 1 engineers, they may be more interested in engine performance and winning the race. Although making money is often a good way to get people's interest, it can also be counterproductive. For example, if you are trying to engage university teaching staff who are steaming about the adverse effect of financial cuts, talking about cost savings will just label you as one of the enemy.

It's very worthwhile to tap into the less obvious motivations too. Fundraisers for charities have to get good at doing this, because fundamentally they are about taking rather than making money. They know that they need to propose projects that fit into the donor's formal criteria for grant giving, but they also try to find a project that hooks into the donor's deeper personal motivations. Although some donors are looking for a permanent memorial (J. Paul Getty's Getty Museum, for example), over half the donors interviewed for the study "Why Rich People Give" had preferred at times to be anonymous, getting their reward instead from the enjoyment of being personally involved in something they felt worthwhile.[149] The study showed that the most important motivations for giving were belief in a cause, being a catalyst for change, self-actualization, a sense of responsibility and the quality of relationships. The quality of relationships was the most important element in determining whether they continued to support the project: people want to feel valued for more than their money.

Even if your idea is a commercial one, paying attention to these more personal motivations will help you get your idea adopted and may well help you get a better financial deal.

5 How (will you make your idea work?)

There are always uncertainties in early-stage ideas. The important thing is not to deny these, or even to attempt to have removed them all, but to have a credible plan for how you will resolve them: for example, building a prototype, doing some market research or trying out the idea on your family and friends. If you are presenting your idea to someone, it's much better to build their trust by pointing out a potential risk area and discussing calmly how you are going to deal with it, rather than let them spot a problem that you hadn't noticed.

Finally, as any salesman knows, you need to try to get them take the next small step towards getting involved. This can be as simple as asking for their opinion, arranging a meeting for further discussions or getting them to sign a petition, but even simple actions get them just a little more engaged in your idea.

The challenge of intuition

For four hours, late into the night of 27 January 1986, two Morton Thiokol engineers, Roger Boisjoly and Arnie Thompson, were in a teleconference trying to convince their management and NASA not to launch the *Challenger* space shuttle the following morning.

They were concerned because the predicted launch temperature, 26–29°F (–2°C to –3°C), was far colder than any previous launch and they had a suspicion that the critical O-ring seals on the booster rocket would seal less effectively at low temperatures. The problem was how to be convincing, when they had no absolute proof and both NASA and Morton Thiokol had a culture that demanded rationality.

The design of the O-ring seal had been tricky, involving a lot of discussion between NASA and Morton Thiokol before they all thought they had a design that could resist the pressures and temperatures it would be exposed to when the booster rocket fired. The design had been steadily improved over the previous launches, so although there were several examples of erosion damage to the seals, it was difficult to disentangle the causes.

When it became clear that the planned launch would be so much colder than any previous launch, they hastily gathered their data. As is so often the case, however, it was difficult to decide exactly at what temperature it would become unsafe, so they chose 53°F: the temperature of the launch with the worst erosion to date. They then called an impromptu teleconference and, for the first time ever, recommended "no launch".

They'd faxed thirteen charts of their data over to NASA and these were intently debated in the teleconference. Understandably, NASA vigorously questioned the justification for the new, and apparently arbitrary, "no launch" temperature threshold.

After nearly four hours, Morton Thiokol asked for five minutes off-line to discuss their position. This turned into half an hour in which Boisjoly and Thompson reiterated their case, while the other engineers present were mostly silent. Finally Jerry Mason, the SVP and chair, said that as engineering could not produce any new information, it was time for management to make

Blow By History

SRM-15 WORST Blow-By
- 2 CASE JOINTS (80°), (110°) Arc
- MUCH WORSE VISUALLY THAN SRM-22

SRM 22 Blow-By
- 2 CASE JOINTS (30-40°)

SRM-13 A, 15, 16A, 18, 23A 24A
- NOZZLE Blow-By

HISTORY OF O-RING TEMPERATURES (DEGREES- F)

MOTOR	MBT	AMB	O-RING	WIND
DM-4	68	36	47	10 mPH
DM-2	76	45	52	10 mPH
QM-3	72.5	40	48	10 mPH
QM-4	76	48	51	10 mPH
SRM-15	52	64	53	10 mPH
SRM-22	77	78	75	10 mPH
SRM-25	55	26	29	10 mPH
			27	25 mPH

Two of the thirteen charts faxed to NASA in support of the "no-launch" recommendation
Reproduced from Edward R. Tufte, *Visual Explanations, images and quantities, evidence and narrative*[150]

a decision – the normal way of resolving differences of opinion amongst the engineers. The four managers present voted to launch, explaining subsequently that they changed their minds because of the lack of data showing a correlation between temperature and blow-by, and because of the safety margin built into the design.

They went back on-line and told NASA, who were somewhat surprised. They'd expected Morton Thiokol to come back with a more reasonable and better justified "no launch" temperature. NASA asked if there were any disagreements or other comments about the recommendation, but no one said anything and the teleconference ended.

The following morning the launch went ahead. The engineers watched on TV. Initially all seemed to be going well and they breathed a huge sigh of relief. They had expected *Challenger* to explode on the launch pad. However, 73 seconds later their worst fears were realized: the booster exploded, killing all seven crew and destroying the myth of an infallible "can do" space programme.

The *Challenger* disaster is sometimes presented as an example of amoral managers overriding honest engineers, but the reality is more complicated. Even though it would have been embarrassing to have missed the launch slot, which was timed to suit the State of the Union address, neither NASA nor Morton Thiokol would have risked destroying the space programme for the sake of it. However, the immediate problem was that there seemed to be no evidence to justify a decision to abort the launch.

The critical charts were produced in only a few hours, so no one would have expected them to be beautifully presented. However, as Edward Tufte, the expert on information design, points out, Boisjoly and Thompson lost the argument because the charts were unconvincing; they had chosen to present the wrong data in the wrong way.[151] Firstly, although they wanted to convince NASA that low temperatures increased the risk of damaged O-rings, none of the charts directly compared the O-ring temperature with the damage. This was a major failing, because it meant that people had to wade through information on several charts, much of which was irrelevant, to find the connection.

Secondly, they threw away most of their data. They were focused on the more serious problem of blow-by, which is when hot gases blow past the primary seal and can threaten the second seal direct rather than just cause minor erosion of the primary seal. The problem was that there were only two examples of this and as one was on a cold day, the other on a warm day, this made a very unconvincing case. However, the picture would have been much clearer if they had included all 24 launches, seven of which had suffered some degree of erosion and seal damage while 17 had not. Critically, these trouble-free launches were all at the higher temperatures, so plotting the amount of damage against the temperature makes the danger of launching at low temperature very clear. It also makes it visually obvious just how much colder the expected launch temperature of 26–29°F was than any previous experience.

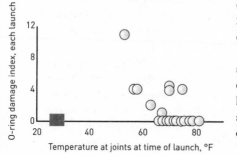

O-ring damage vs launch temperature (grey rectangle is expected temperature at launch)

The engineers' intuition had spotted this pattern hidden in their data, but because they hadn't articulated it and presented it clearly and simply, they failed to convince others.

The wider moral is that when thinking about how to explain an intuitive idea it is very easy to become so focused in on a narrow issue (for example, Boisjoly's two blow-by examples) that you fail to notice the breadth of factors that have helped you realize that the situation is unusual and interesting. By finding a simple way to share your understanding of what is normal and what is not, you make it easier for others to share your insight.

Images

Roger Boisjoly and Arnie Thompson would probably have been more successful in getting their idea across to their colleagues, managers and NASA if they had found a way to represent their intuition visually on a graph.

Images can be much more powerful and memorable than words for conveying ideas because although they seem simple, they can carry more associations than words, and can more easily touch us emotionally as well as rationally. No film producer would dream of producing a film consisting only of subtitles on a blank background, but all too often inventors and creative people try to get their ideas adopted using a Powerpoint presentation, illustrated with at most a clip-art light bulb.

In June 1972 a South Vietnamese aircraft accidentally dropped its load of napalm on the village of Trang Bang. The photo of a young girl running, naked and screaming, down the road out of the village shocked the world, and did much to turn public opinion against the Vietnam War.

The Pulitzer Prize-winning picture was shocking because of the child's nakedness, pain and vulnerability. She was thought of as just "the girl in the picture", and used as a symbol by peace campaigners and the communist regime alike. Seeing her as a "real" person would have destroyed the simplicity of the message, so few knew her name or what happened to her afterwards.

The story of her life is, however, quietly inspiring.[152] The photographer, Nick Ut, took the child, nine-year-old Phan Thi Kim Phuc, to hospital, where to everyone's surprise she survived third degree burns over half her body. When she grew up she studied in Cuba, got married and subsequently moved to Canada. Although she is still in constant pain, she dedicated her life to promoting peace, working with UNESCO, setting up the Kim Foundation, a charity to help child victims of war,[153] and publicly pardoning the person who bombed the village.

Images can also be used to trigger deep-seated mental models to support an idea.

For example, when in 1995 Greenpeace ran their campaign to prevent Shell dumping the redundant Brent Spar oil platform at sea, even they were surprised at the way the campaign caught the public imagination. Spontaneous protests broke out all over Europe, with some Shell petrol stations in Germany reporting a 50% drop in sales. At the eleventh hour, Shell abandoned its plan and towed the platform back to land.

Part of the reason for the campaign's success was the elemental power of

Greenpeace protesters being sprayed by water cannon during their occupation of Shell's
disused Brent Spar oil platform, June 1995   Greenpeace/David Sims

the images, the tiny Greenpeace inflatable battling against fire hoses to protect innocent nature from the vast lump of industrial junk. This was David and Goliath, with Shell in the role of Goliath (big and bad) and Greenpeace as David (small and good).

In 1998 Brent Spar was finally dismantled and used as the base for a new quay in Norway. This probably caused less pollution than dumping it in the deep Atlantic, although the relative merits were debated vigorously for several years. However, the campaign's most significant result was the way it galvanized the whole corporate sector to start paying much more attention to CSR (Corporate Social Responsibility). Corporations suddenly realized that a consumer backlash might be caused by even the perception of bad behaviour.

Images also help turn new and unfamiliar ideas into common sense.

The first way to do this is to link an idea with a person. So, for example, the child Phan Thi Kim Phuc came to symbolize the victims of the Vietnam War. And many more people recognize Einstein's image than understand what his theory of relativity was actually about. Brands try to develop a "persona".

It can be useful to deliberately "promote" someone to symbolize an idea, so even though Al Qaeda is thought to be a network of virtually autonomous groups rather than a hierarchical organization, in the aftermath of the attack on the World Trade Center, portraying Bin Laden as a supreme commander was an attempt to help people grasp the inescapably rather nebulous concept of a "war on terror".

People also understand complex issues more easily from a trusted, familiar face, so TV channels develop and stick with their news anchors, while campaign groups do better if they have a regular spokesperson, particularly if they can find someone with the gift of coming up with good soundbites.

Sometimes it's more feasible to associate an idea with a metaphor than with a person, so, for example, European food surpluses become "butter mountains", wishful thinking is "pie in the sky", an interfering government becomes a "nanny state". Metaphors help make ideas seem real and graspable, but they are also more engaging than a rigorous definition of a concept because they leave room for the imagination.

Ideas are accepted more readily if they seem real and concrete, rather than abstract and theoretical, so the amazing architecture and stained glass of a cathedral helps convey the glory of God. The traditional totem poles of the northwestern United States were probably constructed to help convey social status.

If you work in a nebulous area like "professional services", it can be very helpful to use images and tangible samples to get across the idea of what you do. I was once working with some lawyers who were trying to convey the idea that they weren't just legal experts but used their creativity to help deliver results. One of the techniques that worked best for them was to show prospective clients things to represent their successful assignments, such as the brochure from the property deal or the sample of the successfully licensed invention. These were nice and tangible and so all helped convey the idea that they delivered results for their clients.

It is always hard to choose the right object to use to "concretize" an important and intangible concept, and sometimes people go too far. The concept of human consciousness and the nature of life itself is an intangible idea, so most religions try to make it easier to grasp by talking about the soul as if it were an almost physical entity. However, in the early 1900s a Massachusetts doctor, Duncan McDougall, took this to a bizarre extreme: he weighed dying people and, because his measurements showed that they became slightly lighter at the moment of death, he decided that the soul weighed 21 grams![154]

The power of stories

Stories are much more engaging than a simple presentation.

In February 1996, in the very early days of the Internet, Stephen Denning, an operations manager in the World Bank, was asked by his bosses to "look into the issue of information in our organization".

He wasn't exactly thrilled, because at the time "information" was considered a low-status organizational backwater. However, he was also intrigued, because as an early enthusiast of the PC he had an inkling that the emerging Internet might make interesting things possible. Quite rapidly he realized that they could transform the organization, if only they could develop the IT, the systems and the culture to allow knowledge and best practice to be shared rather than locked into organizational silos. The idea of knowledge sharing seemed so obvious to him, but he had real difficulty getting his colleagues to share his enthusiasm. As he said, "Most of the people couldn't or wouldn't seem to understand an idea that seemed to me so obvious and logical and self-evident. To them the notion was strange and incomprehensible and outlandish, almost contrary to common sense, as if coming from another planet."[155]

The breakthrough came when a colleague at lunch told him a story about a health worker in Zambia that epitomized how knowledge sharing was already working. "In June 1995, a health worker in Kamana, Zambia, logged on to the CDC (Center for Disease Control) website in Atlanta and got the answer to a question on how to treat malaria."

He found that this 29-word story was the key to unlocking people's interest. In contrast to complex presentations, full of jargon, flow charts and abstract generalizations, it was simple and engaging, and sparked the imagination. People started debating how to implement the idea rather than raising objections about the proposed change, and in October 1996, the president announced the launch of an organization-wide strategy of knowledge sharing. This was only eight months from the start of Denning's explorations, a remarkably short timescale for a large bureaucratic organization to adopt a new idea.

What makes a good story? As we might expect from the previous chapters, it must be short, but embody the basic idea. It must connect with things the audience cares about, using their language and mental models. Finally, it must be interesting, containing an element of surprise or something unusual.

The story of the Zambian healthcare worker engaged the staff of the

World Bank because many of them had themselves been in the situation of being in a remote country and being asked important questions to which they didn't have the answer. As a result, people empathized with the protagonist and were stimulated to "co-create" their own personal version of the story. This automatically fitted with their personal mental models and motivations, so stirred them to action.

When trying to sell innovative ideas to technical directors, I often told a true story about the SDS Clic tool-free blade-changing system that we had developed for Bosch jigsaws. This went roughly as follows.

> Dr Odendahl, development director for Bosch Powertools, told me that putting the SDS Clic on the top saw in their range had increased sales of all saws by 20%. Even though most of the saws in the range were totally unchanged, sales increased dramatically, because the sales people were now so fired up by having something innovative and new to talk about that they could sell anything to anyone. It took five years before the first competitor got around the patent.

This resonated with my audience and started them thinking about how nice it would be to be in that position, and what sort of innovation they should develop to trigger the same effect. As I was there in front of them, they also started wondering about whether we could help them get there, which was exactly what I wanted them to start thinking.

Stories and ideas that we "co-create" for ourselves automatically fit with our mental models and engage us, because we feel a sense of involvement, satisfaction, ownership and control. However, imposed ideas are very different. Often they don't fit our mental models. Even if they do, the detailed descriptions and procedures that come with them create a sense of dread and loss of control, rather like the feelings we experience when faced with the instructions for installing a new piece of IT hardware, or assembling flat-pack furniture. We have a sense of foreboding that something will go wrong; somehow the instructions won't be quite right for the situation we will find ourselves in, so we will be left stranded and frustrated, having produced a heap of junk instead of the attractive result illustrated on the box.

Stories get shared if they are interesting. It's tempting to try to define every detail of an idea, but often it's the gaps and uncertainties that get people talking. For example, Greenpeace's Brent Spar campaign stimulated intense debate about whether they were doing the right thing: was disposal on land better than disposal at sea, or not? This debate probably did much to spread interest in the campaign.

Although Greenpeace hadn't intended to stimulate so much controversy, the award-winning peace building charity Peace Direct deliberately stimulates interest in peace issues by circulating its supporters with challenging moral questions for discussion.[156] In their mailing of January 2007, they wrote:

> *Sometimes peace and justice may be in conflict. The International Criminal Court has issued a warrant for the arrest of Joseph Kony, leader of the Lord's Resistance Army, which has ravaged Northern Uganda for over 20 years. But many Ugandans feel they would rather have a peace deal with Kony, which the arrest warrant is jeopardizing. It's make or break for the credibility of the ICC – but should this over-ride the chance of peace? Read these different points of view, and see what you think.*[157]

If you are trying to motivate someone to adopt your idea, it may feel like an alarming loss of control just to tell stories and stimulate debate, but if you do it well it is much more effective than trying to win converts by force.

Vocal opposition, silent supporters

With luck, and if you have a genuinely good idea, your presentations, stories, pictures, demonstrations and diplomacy will start to attract supporters. However, it's very easy not to notice how much support you really have because your supporters are likely to be much quieter about it than your opponents.

You will never attract everyone to your idea. No matter how carefully you have tried to target the idea and your presentations to people's interests, some people will remain frozen, some may still be blind, while others will decide that they actively dislike your idea. This may be for all sorts of reasons, from a fear of loss of face if you succeed, to a genuine conviction that the idea just won't work as well as you claim or will damage their interests. Some of these opponents will be important, so you will need to try to understand why they object to it and try to bring them round, refine your idea, or neutralize them. Others will be irritating, but irrelevant, and can safely be ignored.

It takes courage to persist in the face of opposition, and wisdom to be right in persisting.

In February 2003 Ken Livingstone, Mayor of London, launched London's congestion charging scheme. This followed the lead set by Lee Kuan Yew, who introduced the world's first congestion charging scheme in Singapore in 1975. However, although the economic benefits of the Singapore scheme had been clear for nearly thirty years, apart from a small scheme in Durham, UK, no other city leader had had the courage to follow their example.

As the transport planning consultant Martin Richards discusses in his book, *Congestion Charging in London: The Policy and the Politics*, the London scheme is now recognized as an outstanding success, but few would have predicted this from the initial reactions.[158] It has been responsible for a 30% drop in congestion and a reduction in delays, accidents and pollution as people switched from using the car to public transport. However, it was introduced in the face of vocal opposition from almost all quarters and a media that was at best sceptical, and at worst hostile.

As is so often the case, it was those who were most critical that were most vocal, while supporters were mostly silent or expressed reservations.

The media was overwhelmingly sceptical. The few newspapers that supported the principle, such as *The Economist* and the *Financial Times*, thought Ken Livingstone was taking a gamble. Others, including the *Sun*, *The Times*, the *Daily Telegraph* and the *Daily Mail*, were hostile and far from convinced about the benefits, or unwilling to support such a left-wing politician.

One might have expected that the Labour Government would be supportive, because it had promoted congestion charging when it came to power in 1997 and initiated the exploration of the idea. However, after Ken Livingstone's election as an independent mayor (and his consequent expulsion from the Labour Party), as well as a succession of ministerial changes in the Department of Transport, the government distanced itself from the implementation. It couldn't be seen to be frustrating the mayor's scheme, because that would have called into question its commitment to devolution, but nevertheless it aired a succession of doubts about it. For example, in 2002 the Transport Secretary, Alastair Darling, implied in a BBC Radio 4 interview that Livingstone was anti-car, had failed to obtain public support and had not achieved sufficient improvement in bus and underground services.

Business opinion was divided, with some, such as the CBI (Confederation of British Industry), supporting the principle, but increasingly concerned about the visibility of the benefits to business, while others, such as the FSB (Federation of Small Businesses), were adamantly opposed, seeing it as an unfair flat rate tax.

Even natural supporters of the scheme like the London Cycling Campaign raised objections, believing that the scheme was too limited and the charge should be increased from £5 to £10, and the charging period extended into the evenings and weekends.

Almost alone, the transport and environmental campaigning group

Transport 2000 (now Campaign for Better Transport) described it simply as "the best idea since the London Underground".

Behind the welter of opposition, opinion surveys for TfL (Transport for London) showed that public support and opposition for the scheme were approximately equally balanced.

Ken Livingstone showed visionary leadership, and had the courage to take risks and withstand his critics in the short term in order to achieve a longer-term gain. However, courage and leadership alone would not have been sufficient.

Firstly, Livingstone started with a scheme that was well thought through and fair. It wasn't just the mayor's whim, but was based on a scheme developed and published just prior to his election in 2000 by a group of independent experts.[159] Ken Livingstone gave a lot of attention to delivering noticeable benefits from the scheme – for example, reductions in congestion and improvements in the quality of bus services – and to making sure that it would be efficient and effectively enforced. He was also pragmatic about the technology, deciding that it was better to adopt a system that was less than perfect in that it only allowed vehicles to be charged by the day, rather than delay implementation to provide greater technological sophistication.

Secondly, he set up a good team with sufficient funding and clear authority to get on with the job. This was helped because, as an independent, he had political autonomy and a four-year term until his next election. Unusually for the UK, as Mayor of London he also had authority over all aspects of transport in the city. Critically, he recognized that once the decision to introduce the scheme had been made, it was important to move fast before the initial commitment was eroded away, as it so often is, by persistent opposition, technical difficulties or political change.

Thirdly, he understood the importance of consultation. Although the media was largely critical, his team tried to establish good relations with them, and to help them understand the scheme. They also put a lot of effort into making sure that a very high proportion of people who drove into London were aware of why the scheme was needed, why it was fair, and how it would affect them. In a few cases the scheme was modified to take account of representations by objectors, so, for example, the Freight Transport Association successfully campaigned against the initial plans for a £15 charge for heavy vehicles.

The launch of congestion charging was not without its problems, of course. The day-to-day running of the scheme was handled by Capita, TfL's contractor, and it soon became apparent that there were serious deficiencies in the way that

the scheme was operating, with long delays at the call centre and poor enforce-
ment of penalty payments against people entering the zone without paying.
This led to a renegotiation of Capita's contract and subsequent
improvements.

Nevertheless, the success of the London scheme has spurred other cities
around the world to consider the adoption of congestion charging, and has
made it a politically acceptable component of transport policy.

New ideas are virtually always faced with opposition that is more vocal
than the support. This is because, as the psychologist and former head of the
University of Illinois's Human Factors Division, Professor Christopher
Wickens, points out, we've evolved to be more sensitive to a potential future
loss than a possible gain.[160] This is probably because as hunter gatherers it
would have been very serious to move to a new area in which there was no
game, while moving to an area with more food than the group needed would
have made little difference to its survival.

The voluble opposition makes it very easy to feel that your idea is less
well supported than it is and so get demoralized and give up, as had the
leaders of all the other major cities that had considered introducing congestion charging between 1975 and 2003. In other cases, the sense of opposition
makes people go on the attack, as happened with Wegener's supporters when
they were trying to promote the idea of continental drift. This then just
ramps up the opposition to the idea and makes it more difficult to get it
adopted.

It's important to remain cool and realize that this perception of opposition is often incorrect.

The reason for this was explored by Elisabeth Noelle-Neumann, a prominent German analyst of public opinion, who started her career as a young
journalist in Nazi Germany. She published a series of articles in the 1970s on
the "Spiral of Silence", proposing that most people are reluctant to be out of
step with the majority, and so remain silent when they feel that they are in a
minority. As minority opinion holders start to withdraw from sharing their
opinions, the spiral of silence widens. We have probably all noticed this effect
in meetings, or when finding ourselves amongst a group of people holding
different political views to ourselves.

She proposed that mass media also plays a critical role, particularly where
it is strong and unanimous in giving people a sense of the majority view,
whether or not this is right or wrong. This can have significant effects, so, for
example, in the mid 1960s, according to the opinion polls, support for racial
segregation in America simply disappeared, even in the South, within a few

years of the federal authorities beginning to enforce civil rights measures in earnest. What had once been the dominant opinion in some areas soon became virtually taboo, so people would not admit their views, even if they still held them privately.

Because we have so much emotional commitment to our ideas, it can often be difficult to tell whether the opposition is justified. This means that it is vital to stop at intervals and genuinely consult people about your idea. This is not easy to do, but the process will soften the resistance of your opponents, and help you identify your supporters.

For example, my innovation team was once developing a glaucoma drug delivery device for a big pharmaceutical company, aiming to develop something that was easier for elderly people to use more accurately than a conventional eye-dropper bottle. One of the key engineers at our client, Lee, had already made life so difficult for my predecessor that we'd had to take him off the project; I had come in as the replacement project leader to try to get the project back on track.

My first task was to try to understand Lee's problem. He produced a whole list of technical concerns, but I also had the sense that he felt threatened by our project in some way. I couldn't work out quite why, and it was only much later that it became clear that he had his own competing idea for how to solve the problem, and so bitterly resented our involvement.

I did everything I could to involve Lee in the project, get his opinion, incorporate his ideas and be very explicit in giving him credit for them. This worked well enough to let the project get moving again, so some months later I went over to the USA to present the results and demonstrate the device we had come up with. This was an important meeting, as various chief executives were present, including my own.

To my surprise, halfway through the presentation, Lee went on the attack. It went on and on, and it became clear that he had been lying to me and playing politics for weeks. I vigorously held my ground, trying to stay cool, but wishing he would explode in a ball of flame. It was only later, when I reviewed what had happened with my colleagues, that I realized everyone else in the room had been on my side, but had just been waiting for the opportunity to show it. My chief executive said, "If only you'd turned to us and said 'Does anyone else agree with this?' we'd all have come out in your support."

Lee's behaviour was very frustrating, but it probably damaged his credibility more than ours. A few months later, I was told that all Lee's colleagues considered him totally impossible to work with, and he'd just been made redundant. It was hard not to feel vindicated.

In the heat of battle, it's not easy to stop and give your supporters space to identify themselves, but if you can summon up the courage to do so it's very effective, because you almost invariably get more support than you expected. In a meeting this can be as simple as asking people to raise their hands in a straw poll. However, it's much more revealing than a simple poll if you go round in a circle, asking people to give their opinion on the question at hand (or say "pass" if they have nothing to add to what has already been said). This is very effective and still quite quick, especially if people are limited to just one sentence each. For example, if you asked "What do you think of the idea for electric roller skates?", a parent might think the idea would be fun, but worry about safety. An engineer might feel intuitively comfortable that it could be made safe, but worry about how to design it with enough battery life to be fun. A "yes/no" poll asking people to vote whether to go ahead or not might have given the comfortable feeling of producing a quantifiable result, but would have wasted the depth of the collective insight available to improve the idea. This is of course much easier to do if you have a good facilitator involved in your meeting.

Whichever tactic you use, switching the mood from combative to reflective, and giving voice to the silent majority, totally changes the feeling of the meeting and helps convert people from being passive recipients into active, engaged participants.

Integrated

"We've always done it this way"

In the fourth and final stage, the idea that was once new has to become integrated into people's personalities, behaviour and daily lives, to become part of the normal way that they do things and think about things, to seep into their mental models.

Unfortunately this process of integration doesn't happen automatically.

Even when people do support your idea, their initial enthusiasm can fade frustratingly fast, so, for example, they come out of a training course determined to change, but within a few weeks the pressures of life have overwhelmed their enthusiasm and the idea is quietly forgotten. This gets frustrating, because you think you've won someone over, then a few weeks later you discover that they have done nothing about it.

In this final stage, as discussed in this chapter, the challenge is to persist, steadily helping people integrate the idea in their own lives and widening the circle of support. This may feel less fun than the dramatic demonstrations, presentations and interventions of the earlier stages, but you will know you have finished when people start to forget that things were ever different.

They will say, "We've always done it this way."

They may not remember where the idea came from, but you will be able to look on your work with pride.

Embedding your ideas

When you feel that people agree with your ideas, it's very easy to relax in the warm glow of appreciation. But if you do, the ideas will wither and die.

Ideas won't stick until they have been integrated into people's mental models, personality, relationships and behaviour, but this takes effort, so it's more likely to happen if you or your supporters can provide the reinforcement, support and feedback to help it along.

Reinforcement and support

There are several ways of helping people integrate new ideas into their lives. The first and most basic is to keep reminding them, so, for example, marketers use "retrieval cues" to remind shoppers in supermarkets about the adverts they saw on TV the night before. Sales people make follow-up calls.

Secondly, new ideas need support before they will become embedded.

Often this is essential, because most ideas don't work very well initially. For example, although today photocopiers and printers jam occasionally, the early copiers were much more frustrating to use. Not only was paper feeding unreliable and the print quality variable, but some types were even supplied with a fire extinguisher because they used a heated, inflammable liquid toner and were liable to catch fire.

When Xerox developed their dry-toner system, it had the advantage that copying was faster and cheaper than its competitors (and it was less likely to catch fire), but the machines were expensive and complex and still tended to be unreliable. Xerox cleverly got round this by developing a new business model, in which they rented the machines for a fee based on the number of copies made, but included "free" service, parts and ink. This made their customers much more accepting of the unreliability, and so by the 1960s Xerox was the fastest growing company in US history.

Your idea may not have the commercial impact of the photocopier, but if someone is interested in your idea, don't just give them a sample and hope they'll love it, but find an excuse to pop in and say, "How's it going?"

That will give them permission to admit that they couldn't work out how to switch it on (this happened with the design of a new MP3 player my team was once involved in) or have got hung up on some detail they don't like. You can then listen to any concerns, deal with the problems, and leave them feeling valued, involved, and much more likely to persist in trying out your idea.

Good technical support helps people accept the unreliability of innovative products. Similarly, good social networks help people overcome the unpredictable challenges of doing new things.

In the UK, the failure rate for new small businesses is 20–30% within the first year. Being entrepreneurial can be a tough and lonely game, particularly when, as so often happens with new ideas, things don't work out the way you expect and your backers start getting worried. However, it can be much easier for small entrepreneurs in Bangladesh.

The Grameen Bank started at the University of Chittagong, Bangladesh, in 1976 when Professor Muhammad Yunus launched a research project on how to provide banking for the poor. From this came the principle of microfinance lending, lending small sums (never more than a few hundred dollars) to small groups of five non-related individuals who mutually guarantee the

Women at a weekly collection meeting in Bangladesh, repaying loans funded by the Grameen Bank
© Shehzaad Nourani/Still Pictures

loan. Typically they use the money to buy looms, chickens or cows, or make small capital investments.

This has been an extremely successful idea: it is estimated that the income of households taking the loans is about 50% higher than similar households in other villages, while as few as 3% default on the loan. By 2007, Grameen Bank had lent over $5 billion, had seven million borrowers and had stimulated other institutions to set up micro-finance projects round the world.

Muhammad Yunus and the Grameen Bank jointly received the Nobel Peace Prize in 2006.

The project has been so successful in helping people who would not otherwise be able to get financial backing because of the way it uses peer support: the key feature of the programme is that a candidate for a loan must form a group with four other people who are not family members. Two members of the group get a loan first, and if they do well, the others then receive loans. The borrowers are encouraged to assist each other, and all loans and repayments are made publicly, in front of other groups. Loans are always for one year, at a fixed interest rate substantially lower than that charged by the money lenders.

The mutual guarantee means that there's an incentive for people to recruit other good borrowers to join them and for the members of the group to monitor and support each other, sometimes even helping with things like education or insurance. Grameen Bank is also efficient because the transaction costs are relatively low. Unlike a conventional bank, where highly paid "professionals" try to use algorithms and procedures to guess whether the money will be repaid, the members of a micro-finance group are in a much better position to know whether someone's being lazy or is having a run of bad luck, and much more motivated to help fix any problems before it's too late.

In the same way, if you can build your own network of constructive, challenging supporters, you will have a much better chance of getting your idea to really fly.

Many of us have the social skills to develop our own support networks if we really want to, but if you are trying to change the way other people think and behave, it will help if you can provide that support for them.

For example, the two Ipswich tenancy support workers referred to in Chapter 5 were a vital part of the success of the programme to reduce the number of evictions, because they were there as supportive friends to help the tenants cope with the inevitable crises over the first year or two as they got used to the idea of using a calendar.

A more extreme example comes from the treatment and control of sex offenders.

Their offences are so deep rooted that it's particularly hard to persuade them to change their beliefs and habits. However, one programme does seem to be being successful in dealing with it. This is the idea of "Circles of Support and Accountability" developed in Canada in 1994, when Mennonite pastor Harry Nigh was approached by a prison psychologist asking if he could help with Charlie Taylor, a repeat, mentally retarded sex offender who was about to be released into his community. Even though the area was in uproar, with Taylor's picture put up on posters on the lampposts, Harry Nigh got together four members of his congregation and invited them to dinner to see if they could help Charlie Taylor settle in the community. The group grew, and, initially calling themselves "Charlie's angels", regularly met Taylor. They made sure he was taking his medication and monitored him, while involving him in the church and community. This kept the community far safer than the police could ever have done because initially someone would be meeting him every day, with a meeting with the group every seven days. The support continued until Charlie Taylor's death twelve years later, and he never re-offended.

This grew into a programme that is now in every major city in Canada and spreading around the world. It was recently the subject of a very successful three-year trial in the Thames Valley in the UK, run by the Quakers in conjunction with the Home Office, and is now spreading across other areas of the UK.[161]

The version of the system that is used in the UK is intended as a final stage of the statutory framework for dealing with offenders, and so is fairly formal. Offenders have started by going through a sex offender treatment programme, usually before they are released from prison. This "unfreezes" them by confronting them with the harm they have done. Once they are "interested" they are helped to think through how they want to change to avoid temptation in the future. They are also asked to make a plan for the "integration" stage, which includes questions like, "Who will help you live up to this?"

It is often very hard for the offenders to identify anyone to help them, other than an overstretched probation officer, because they have frequently been in prison for many years and are not allowed to return to their original communities, as they would be isolated and ostracized if they did. In many cases too, they have very low self-esteem and hence find it difficult to build the circle of friends that most of us manage to do for ourselves. As a result, even though they may have left prison determined not to go back, many fail to resist the temptation all around them and offend again.

If they volunteer to join a Circle of Support and Accountability, each offender becomes the "core member" of a group, and is supported by a group of four or five volunteers who commit to meet them over at least a year, typically once a week. The groups are in turn supported by a member of staff. The volunteers have to make a significant commitment in time and energy, but organizers find that every time there is some publicity about the programme, they get a steady stream of people volunteering to help. Just as the offenders' crimes are shocking, so people are motivated to try to help prevent them. About a quarter of the volunteers are themselves victims of child abuse.

The fundamental principles of the circles are threefold: to provide support by reducing loneliness, modelling appropriate behaviour and demonstrating humanity; to protect the community by monitoring what the offender is doing; and to maintain the relationship and treatment programme. This combination is very successful, so in the first five years of the UK programme, none of the thirty offenders had committed a new offence. Offenders say that one of the key driving factors is that "The volunteers are giving their time to me. I don't want to let them down."

This sense of obligation is a powerful motivation for keeping up with difficult things, whether it's supporting relatives in need or working to pay back a loan from a friend.

Few ideas are as hard to get fully adopted as getting a paedophile to change, but when thinking about your own idea, it's important to consider what support it will need to become fully adopted, and how this will be provided. For some ideas, all that will be needed is technical help to deal with occasional problems and to stop people getting frustrated. However, if you want to get ideas adopted that challenge fundamental and deep-rooted assumptions, you will need to provide deeper and more personal support.

Feedback, rewards and sanctions

The third aspect of embedding ideas is to provide the feedback, rewards and sanctions to help motivate the behaviour you want.

If you are struggling to get your boss to stick with a promise of delegating authority to you, you can help make the new idea stick by first doing a good job when he does delegate: making a mess will just reinforce his previous beliefs and anxieties about your abilities. Second, make sure he knows you're pleased when he does the right thing. This very simple feedback will help reinforce the behaviour pattern you want.

It may also be useful to stop him jumping to inaccurate conclusions. As we saw in Chapter 4, one of the mechanisms for blindness is that we force-fit our perceptions into our mental models. This causes problems when we are trying to get someone to absorb new ideas, because they will very often force-fit what they observe into their out of date mental models, thus reinforcing the old model, not the new one.

This can produce the most amazing misinterpretations of events. I was once working with a development group at a major food manufacturer, helping them get more effective at turning their ideas into reality. At one point the manager, Gavin, said of a recent big project, "Jane [the project leader] hated it."

Shortly afterwards I met Jane, who was clearly getting frustrated and feeling micro-managed by Gavin. When I asked her how she'd felt about the project, far from saying she hated it she said, "It was hell but brilliant... The most rewarding thing I've ever done."

Jane was energetic, creative and not afraid to speak her mind, so I can well believe that Gavin heard all too much about the "hell" side of it, then jumped to the wrong conclusion about the sort of work Jane liked, and how she wanted to be managed. However, when, with encouragement from me, Jane sat down with Gavin and told him how much she'd enjoyed the project and why, it transformed her career.

People respond to feedback, whether it's a reward for doing the right thing, sanctions for doing the wrong thing or simply information on how they are doing on something that they care about.

As we saw in Chapter 6, if people are frozen they will only take action if the psychological rewards seem greater than the costs. This also applies in the later stages, so your supporters will rapidly drift away if you ask them to do boring or seemingly pointless things, like attend endless coordination meetings or work with no feedback on progress.

As we saw in Chapter 5, when dealing with creative ideas the rewards that are most important and motivating are often not the immediate financial ones, but rather things like interest, fulfilment or status. These foster our sense of intrinsic motivation; we feel we are doing things just because we want to, not because someone else wants us to. This then makes us more creative, more open to ideas, and helps people trust us when we enthuse about the idea. We all probably recognize the contrast in how we respond when a friend is buzzing about a great idea, or we're called by a stranger from a call centre reading a script and trying to sell us something.

There has been some fascinating research recently on why people devote their time and expertise for free in building participative websites like YouTube, MySpace or Wikipedia. These sites are sometimes known as "Web 2.0" and adopt the principle of trusting users as "co-developers", harnessing their collective intelligence to produce something that gets better the more people get involved.

The psychologist and head of Stanford University's Persuasive Technologies Lab, B. J. Fogg, points out that websites like Flickr or YouTube are so successful (at least until the copyright lawyers get involved) not only because they make it very easy to post a video and share links, but because they reward behaviour that enhances the website. This encourages people to move on from simple discovery of the website to become actively engaged. He says, "The secret is to tie the acquisition of friends, compliments and status – spoils that humans will work hard for – to activities that enhance the site, such as inviting new users and contributing photos. You offer someone a context for gaining status, and they are going to work for that status."[162]

The photo-sharing website Flickr assigns images an "interestingness" score depending on how many people view them and whether they comment. This helps the site because it can then give top ranking to the most popular photos, and it encourages people to email their friends with the link. Good websites keep people involved by giving them rewards, so bloggers get comments from their readers and YouTube users come back to check if they've moved up the rankings.

The "Open Source" community has developed some remarkably professional software, even though (or perhaps because) it's virtually all done by unpaid volunteers, producing results that are designed to be publicly and freely available, rather than protected by copyright and patents. Wikipedia has become a widely used resource, covering quite controversial topics in a remarkably thorough and balanced way. Open-source software like Linux is more stable and bug-free than Microsoft, so in 2004, over 65% of website servers used open-source Apache software. I was told by one Microsoft insider a few years ago that even Microsoft was using open-source software to run its internal servers.

The political economist Steven Weber explores why people choose to get involved in his book, *The Success of Open Source*. About one third of respondents to a 2001 survey by the Boston Consulting Group were "believers", motivated by the conviction that software (or knowledge) should be freely available.[163] A quarter did it for fun, and a fifth were doing it because it helped them with their jobs, or helped them learn new skills.

A major motivation to get involved is because it's interesting and rewarding. They see something wrong, whether it's a software bug or an inaccuracy on Wikipedia, and want to fix it. As they put it, they want to "scratch the itch". Open-source project managers say that the secret of success in managing their volunteers is to "make it interesting, and make sure it happens".

Whereas programmers' work in companies is often invisible and unappreciated, getting involved in an open-source project can be an opportunity to learn new skills and demonstrate their ability in an environment in which good work is appreciated by people who know what they are looking at, while bad code is mercilessly taken apart. As one might expect, this means that open-source projects tend to attract better programmers than average.

People respond to people, so if you are trying to use the Web to gather supporters for your idea, beware the temptation to send out automated responses and mass mailings. It will be more effective if people can see and share their own work, working within the framework you have set up.

You can use similar processes offline to give people the continuing flow of subtle rewards and feedback that will help keep them motivated.

Bill Bratton, the New York Police Department chief, had opened his senior staff's eyes to the need to reduce petty crime on the subway by forcing them to travel on it. However, he knew this wouldn't be enough on its own to make the idea stick, so he followed it up with various new processes to reinforce the change. One of these was the institution of a strategic review meeting every two weeks, at which one of the precinct commanders had to give a detailed report to about a hundred of his peers and bosses. This kept everyone on their toes because they only got two days' notice, and knew that high achievers would be recognized, while incompetent commanders could no longer get away with blaming their failings on their neighbouring precincts, because the other commanders would be right there in the room. These meetings helped change the culture of the organization, encouraging commanders to share experiences, something that had very seldom happened before.

I've found that this simple principle of starting a meeting by asking people to give a brief update on progress and problems can be a very effective way to help create an open, collaborative atmosphere.

It would be nice to think that the beauty of your idea would be enough on its own to make the idea spread. This may work initially, but even the most altruistic and worthwhile idea will be vulnerable to being killed off by people acting more selfishly.

For example, when Tim Berners-Lee invented the World Wide Web at

CERN in Switzerland, the world's largest particle physics laboratory, he made his idea available freely, with no patent and no royalties due. In 1994 he founded the World Wide Web Consortium of companies to improve it, and again they decided that their standards would be based on royalty-free technology, so they could be easily adopted by anyone. Their altruism transformed the way we share knowledge and contributed to the huge growth of the Internet, but others were not as altruistic. By 2006 an estimated 86% of emails were unwanted spam and the system is creaking under the strain.[164] This is leading to a debate about whether it's time to institute a system for charging for sending emails, but the design of the system makes this difficult and many IT insiders feel passionately that it's against the original "spirit of the Internet".[165]

Having some form of sanctions against "rule breakers" can be very important in preserving the beauty of the idea: people might not have welcomed the idea of the London Congestion Charging scheme, but they wouldn't have accepted it as generally fair if people who entered the zone without paying weren't charged a penalty.

It turns out that sanctions become particularly important as the group size increases. The economist Herbert Gintis of the University of Massachusetts and the anthropologist Robert Boyd of the University of California at Los Angeles got interested in how cooperation could have evolved. To explore this, they set up a computer simulation in which the individuals were programmed either to cooperate or to cheat on each other, but also to copy successful behaviour.[166] They were then put into groups that were allowed to compete. This showed that small groups of fewer than about ten people did better the more cooperators there were in the group. Cooperation only emerged in groups of up to fifty individuals if they added a third category of people, the punishers, or people who would punish people who cheated. Subsequent research showed that cooperation can become the default behaviour in large groups of several hundred people, provided that the punishers are willing to punish not only those who cheat, but also those who fail to punish cheats.[167]

These experiments were only a computer model, but the results fit with our experience of groups: small groups are most likely to cooperate freely and naturally, and are most receptive to new ideas, and most creative, brainstorming sessions work best with fewer than ten people. As the group grows beyond about fifty – for example, as a young business grows – it's still buzzy but it needs to become a little more hierarchical and disciplined, with managers and teams, typically of up to about twelve people. As it grows above about 150–200, things change once again; people don't even recognize everybody, so formal systems start taking over from trust and informal cooperation.

Stepping back

As will by now be clear, developing a creative idea requires independence, persistence and the strength of mind to carry on when people are telling you the idea's impossible. However, people will only truly adopt an idea and integrate it into their own lives and mental models when they feel that in some way they "own" it too. The more egotistical and controlling you are about insisting that it's "your" idea, perfect and fully formed, the more difficult it will be to get it adopted. If, on the other hand, you can start to think of it as a child that is growing up, and that needs its own freedom to develop in ways you can't and mustn't control, you will be much more successful.

Many creative people find this transition difficult. This is a shame because it means that good ideas take far longer than necessary to get adopted, or only get adopted after their creator has died. A good example of this is in the very different approaches adopted by Copernicus and Galileo in trying to getting the idea of a sun-centred "heliocentric" universe adopted.

Copernicus had first described his ideas about the heliocentric hypothesis in 1514, in a text circulated to friends. By 1536 rumours were reaching educated people all over Europe. Many people, including the Archbishop of Capua, Nikolaus Cardinal von Schönberg, were urging him to publish. He remained cautious, but his work, *De revolutionibus*, was finally published when he was on his deathbed in 1543. Over the next twenty years, more than 600 copies were printed, a huge number for the time.

Recent research, tracking down all surviving copies, shows that many of them were owned by the top scientists of the time and were annotated in the margins; the ideas were clearly being widely discussed and circulated in a sixteenth-century equivalent of email.

Initially the work did not get much reaction from the religious authorities. This was partly because Copernicus had been careful to cultivate good relations with them: *De revolutionibus* included a delicately worded dedication to Pope Paul III, which undoubtedly helped reduce resistance. The book also included a preface inserted anonymously by the book's overseer, Andreas Osiander, stating that the system was a pure mathematical device and was not supposed to represent reality. This was probably directly contrary to Copernicus's personal Neoplatonist views, but helped soften resistance amongst scientists. Because Copernicus was assuming that the planets moved in perfect circles (rather than ellipses as realized later by Kepler), the predictions of the heliocentric theory were still far from a perfect match with observations.

Some people, including John Donne and William Shakespeare, feared Copernicus's theory, feeling that it destroyed the hierarchal natural order, and would in turn destroy social order and bring about chaos. As we discussed in Chapter 4, our mental models are indeed very interconnected!

It was only sixty years later that the idea of the heliocentric universe became firmly seen as heretical, when Galileo began his so-called Copernican crusade. The Catholic Church's opposition grew steadily, and in 1616 Galileo was banned from holding or defending heliocentric views. Galileo was tried for heresy in 1633, accused of disobeying this order, and spent the remaining nine years of his life under house arrest.

The Professor of Ethics and Rector of the Martin Bucer Seminary in Bonn, Thomas Schirrmacher, points out that many of Galileo's problems were not fundamentally because of religious opposition, as by then it had been well accepted that the planets went around the sun, even if it was not yet agreed whether the Earth moved.[168] He met much stronger resistance than Copernicus in part because he lived in different times, with a cruel and political pope. However, Galileo also made things more difficult for himself. He directly attacked the pope, who found it particularly provoking that these attacks were in Italian rather than the usual Latin, so that even non-scholars could read them. Galileo's stubborn and arrogant personality also amplified the resistance from the scientific community. The Hungarian polymath Arthur Koestler pointed out that "Galileo had a rare gift of provoking enmity; not the affection alternating with rage which Tycho aroused, but the cold, unrelenting hostility which genius plus arrogance minus humility creates among mediocrities."[169]

Galileo was a great scientist, but his arrogance and intellectual selfishness were truly spectacular. For example, Galileo wrote to a friend, "You cannot help it, Mr Sarsi, that it was granted to me alone to discover all the new phenomena in the sky and nothing to anybody else. This is the truth which neither malice nor envy can suppress."

He refused to discuss his findings with other scientists and ignored their ideas. In 1609 the German mathematician Johannes Kepler published his *Astronomia nova* showing that the planets moved round the sun in elliptical orbits, not circles, but Galileo ignored this important piece of work and so some of his teachings were already out of date when they were banned.

If we compare Copernicus's and Galileo's progress in getting people to accept the revolutionary idea of a heliocentric universe, Copernicus's diplomacy was much more effective than Galileo's arrogance. While Copernicus let his ideas be pulled out of him, Galileo piled on the pressure. This ramped up the opposition to the extent that he risked torture and death at the hands of the Inquisition, and his works were banned for 200 years.

While Copernicus's *De revolutionibus* was only banned briefly, from 1616 to 1620, the Vatican's ban on Galileo's *Dialogues* remained in place until 1835.

One might think that the penalty for diplomacy would be invisibility, but in some cases the opposite is true. Perhaps one of the most striking examples of this is the Marshall Plan in the late 1940s.

When in 1947 General George Marshall proposed an initiative to provide aid for the reconstruction of Europe after the devastation of the Second World War, he kept it deliberately low-key.[170]

There was no master plan; Marshall's speech had just the right degree of vagueness to require European action, yet the right degree of specificity to excite it. He insisted that the programme come from Europe and be open to all European states willing to abide by the rules. And to help ensure that the proposal was low-key, it was deliberately announced at a graduation ceremony (hastily arranged at Harvard), on the basis that no one paid attention to them, although various influential British opinion-makers were tipped off that there was going to be a statement on foreign aid.

In contrast to Truman's controversial "Truman Doctrine", Marshall refused to call his initiative the Marshall Plan; it was only later that his name was attached to it.

From 1948 to 1952, America provided $13 billion (worth roughly $130 billion today) to nearly all European countries in the form of direct aid, loan guarantees, grants and other necessities, ranging from medicine to mules.

In 1953, George Marshall won the Nobel Peace Prize.

Reflections

IF WE WAIT FOR THE WORLD to beat a path to our door, we may have a long and lonely wait.

However, we will have a much better chance of getting our ideas adopted if we have the courage to be proactive, and the flexibility to work in very different ways with people in the four stages of resistance. Not only will many more people be "blind" or "frozen" about our ideas than we think, but, to get any significant idea adopted, we will have to work with people who have very different mental models and concerns.

This book has discussed examples from many fields, including technological innovation, social change and business. It may seem a strange mixture to some, but this is often how things are: technology, changing social attitudes and business all interact with each other. Mobile phones were a technological innovation, but they have transformed the way we socialize with our friends. No longer needing to make laborious arrangements for where and when to meet, we just say, "I'll call you when I get there."

More importantly, mobile phones are becoming a way for people in Africa without bank accounts to transfer money back to their villages.[171] This is because they are expensive to use, but so popular that prepaid, pay-as-you-go airtime is becoming a form of currency and savings. Because it can be bought by one person and sent to another with a simple text message, it's a much safer and cheaper way of transferring money than previously, when often the only way to do it was to give a bus driver who was going to the village an envelope of cash with the obvious risk that it would get "lost".

In 2007, Reuters launched a commercial service to middle-income farmers in Maharashtra State, India, supplying text messages with location-specific and crop-related news, price and weather information.[172] This helps farmers take the gamble out of when to sow, when to reap, and where to sell, but also helps Reuters get established in a new business area with a potentially huge market. There are about 120 million farmers in India in the target group (farmers with an income of about $2000 p.a.).

Reuters's experience also demonstrates the way in which ideas need to adapt and change to suit their context. As the Global Head of Innovation, Amanda West, says, "So many of our assumptions just weren't right at the outset."

When the idea had been dreamed up in the corporate headquarters in London, Reuters had assumed that they would be supplying Indian farmers with the same sort of commodities news and global-futures prices that they supplied to traders in the West. However, during the pilot project they very rapidly discovered that a semi-literate Indian farmer isn't interested in the price of wheat on the Chicago Mercantile Exchange; he wants prices much nearer home. As a result, Reuters now employ a network of observers in local markets across the state, feeding information into an IT system that automatically sends each subscriber the local weather forecast and current crop prices at their six nearest markets.

The history of the development of the mobile phone and text messaging is another demonstration of some of the key elements of virtually all successful innovations. It involved an intuitive hunch that text messaging might be useful for something, but also rigorous attention to detail and the need to overcome the various stages of resistance.

When text messaging became available, initially most people were blind to it. They either didn't even notice that the facility existed, or didn't see why anyone would want to use it. After a bit, people became aware that you could send a text message, but found it rather tedious to do, so seldom sent them. Many over-50s are still in this position, but for most younger people, texting has become totally integrated into their lives, to the extent that it is even changing human anatomy. One survey in Japan showed that for the "thumb generation" of people under 25, the thumb has become the strongest and most dextrous digit, to the extent that it is used for tasks like pointing that would, in the past, have been done with a finger.

Just as people start texting because their friends are doing so, we are more likely to adopt ideas if we feel that other people are doing so and can interact with them about it. If someone tries to force us to adopt an idea we are likely to resist on principle.

This book has deliberately focused on a wide range of ideas, from scientific discoveries to humanitarian campaigns. My bias in selecting examples has been to choose ones that I thought would be interesting or inspiring for

people who are in some small way trying to make the world a better place. ˙
do have to admit, however, that the ideas in the book can just as easily be
used to promote useless, foolish or even immoral ideas. It's up to you, the
reader, to decide.

It takes patience and persistence to get ideas adopted, but good ideas
spread faster in some fields than others. Ideas can spread very fast in tightly
structured fields like mathematics or physics, which are governed by strict
laws and logic. When in 1995 the Cambridge mathematician Andrew Wiles
solved Fermat's last theorem, described as the most important mathematical
discovery of the twentieth century, it electrified the mathematical community immediately.[173] On the other hand, ideas that will disrupt important
mental models in less structured fields like philosophy or social science may
take decades or even centuries to get fully integrated. It took Europeans at
least 1,600 years longer than the Chinese to recognize sunspots for what they
were. The idea of continental drift took at least 350 years to get adopted,
from the time at which it was visually obvious that Latin America and Africa
must once have fitted together.

The idea of human-induced climate change is going through this transition at the moment. However, as scientists say that we only have about ten
years to stop the growth in our carbon emissions, we will need to adopt and
act on an important idea faster than at any previous time in human history.

This is a major challenge, but I do not despair. The changing climate is
inevitably going to give us many different shocks to unfreeze us, while the
Internet now allows ideas to spread around the world in a way that was
inconceivable even fifty years ago. We also have the unprecedented resource
of the Intergovernmental Panel on Climate Change (IPCC), which for the
first time in history provides a means for the world's scientists to develop
and report their consensus view. It's up to us all to listen and act, and to give
our politicians the courage and motivation to act too.

The myth suggests that the world will beat a path to your door and heap
fame and riches on your head. However, the reality is very different. Far from
feeling excited (or relieved) when at last your ideas are adopted, it's very easy
to feel flat at this point. Things go quiet, the professionals move in and it's
much less fun than the excitement of the early days, when you were working
all night getting the idea to work, or persuading people to march through the
streets in support of your campaign.

The idea may also have changed quite a bit from your original vision, because
there will have been so many unexpected problems to overcome. So many
people will have been involved that it will be sheer chance who gets the credit.

Francis Crick, James Watson and Maurice Wilkins received the Nobel Prize in 1962 for the discovery of the helical structure of DNA, the most important biological discovery of the twentieth century. It is now widely recognized that their work was based on the work of Rosalind Franklin, a brilliant molecular biologist and crystallographer, who sadly died of cancer four years earlier aged only 37.

Our desire for a simple story with a simple "hero" means that very often one individual will be singled out as the figurehead to symbolize the much more complex reality.

William Wilberforce was credited with getting a bill passed by the British Parliament to abolish the Slave Trade in 1807, but the campaign was started by a small group of Quakers who set up the Committee on the Slave Trade in 1783, four years before Wilberforce became involved. This led the way for the setting up of the Society for the Abolition of the Slave Trade by Granville Sharp and Thomas Clarkson in 1787. Most of the society's members were Quakers, supported by influential figures such as John Wesley and the manufacturer Josiah Wedgwood. They decided they needed a sympathetic advocate for the cause, and found one in Wilberforce.

While Wilberforce was busy in Parliament, Thomas Clarkson travelled the country gathering facts and supporters, which ultimately resulted in 300,000 people supporting a sugar boycott, organized by the abolition movement to hit the profits of the West Indies trade. Many of these protesters were British women, who could not vote, but could make their views felt by refusing to buy the products of slavery. Nevertheless, it took a further 26 years and several slave revolts before transatlantic slavery itself was abolished in the British colonies.

If you have done your job well, by the end the idea may be so well integrated that the world at large may not even be aware that you were involved. You alone, however, will still be able to look at your work and say, "That's my baby."

Yes, it's grown up now, left home, and it's living its own life. You know you can't and mustn't try to control it, but you can still care about its progress and look on its achievements with pride.

As the anthropologist Margaret Mead often said in her various ways, "Never doubt that a small group of thoughtful committed citizens can change the world. Indeed it is the only thing that ever has."[174]

24 Principles

I HOPE YOU HAVE FOUND INTERESTING and useful ideas in this book. However, as should now be clear, these ideas will fade unless you try hard to integrate them into your life.

To help you do this, this section is to let you note down the ideas from the book that you find most useful. I've included my favourites, but your choice will depend on your personality, experience, environment and ideas.

My favourites	Your favourites
1 The myth of the mousetrap	
Resistance is normal – so don't get demoralized, get smart	
Creative ideas are as involving as beliefs.	
Make people feel involved, not coerced.	
2 Understanding our creativity	
Value both intuitive insights and rational analysis.	
Know your personality, recognize and address your weaknesses.	
Relish impossibilities, but not in yourself.	

My favourites	Your favourites

3 Engaging with reality

Focus on the objective, hold the space.

Look for the non-obvious unmet need.

Value and question your constraints.

4 Blind

Mental models are invisible, important and hard to change.

They differ profoundly between groups.

If our perceptions don't fit our mental models, we either filter them out, or force-fit them until they do.

5 Opening their eyes

Combine the familiar with the unexpected.

Trigger more helpful mental models.

Make sure your "surprises" are interpreted the way you want.

6 Frozen

Provide clear evidence of the need to change.

Make people care.

Give them the safety to care.

7 Interested

Be visionary, but realistic.

Connect with people's interests.

Use images and stories to share your intuitions, use data and facts to support them.

My favourites	Your favourites

8 **Integrated**

Persist.

Provide support, reinforcement and feedback.

Feel good when others start evolving and "owning" your idea.

The ideas in this book can be applied in many different ways, so do share your experiences at www.annemiller.info

Acknowledgements

AS MY HUSBAND, TOM, quite correctly pointed out, I didn't really have time to write this book, so my first thanks are to him for being unfailingly supportive and patient in putting up with all the things that got displaced by the process of writing. His insightful comments and questions helped me transform my half-formed ideas and drafts into a coherent whole.

The book would never have existed without Alastair Barber, who got me to write an article entitled "The Myth of the Mousetrap" for The East of England Development Agency; Tim Bates of Pollinger, who saw that it would make a book; and Martin Liu of Cyan, who agreed. They all played a major role in making it happen. Jeremy Waller and Ursula Lennel nobly read the whole book in draft form, making perceptive and useful comments. I am also indebted to Noam Cook, Daniel Simons, Juliet Freeman, Peter Miller, Rosemary Randall, Tony Hooley, Peter Fenwick, Kevin Holley, Devon Polachek, Tony Quayle, Andy Jones, Hugh Parnell, John Stanton, Noriko Sasaki, Michael Bradley, Rita Carter, Mike Shur, Paul Forty and Alan Hallett, who all helped. It hardly needs saying that I am of course responsible for all errors, omissions and other weaknesses.

I would also like to thank all my other clients, colleagues and friends who, knowingly or not, have contributed to the book.

My thoughts have been influenced by many of the sources listed in the references, but a few have been particularly important in developing my thinking. Ed Schein's work on transformative change is illuminating, and is described in much more depth than it is here in several of his books, including *Process Consultation* and *Corporate Culture: A Survival Guide*. The discussion of the cultural differences in Chapter 4 would have been much weaker without Richard Nisbett's fascinating book *The Geography of Thought*, while Jared Diamond's book *Collapse* gives much more detail on the Inuit and the

Vikings in Greenland. Harry Collins and Trevor Pinch's book *The Golem at Large* provided the source material for the discussion of the AIDS activists in Chapter 5 and contributed to the discussion of the *Challenger* disaster, while Edward Tufte pointed out how the disaster could have been averted in his wonderful book *Visual Explanations*. Martin Richard's book *Congestion Charging in London* provided me with the information for the story told in Chapter 7.

I wish to thank the individuals and organizations listed below for permission to reproduce copyright material that has not been acknowledged elsewhere. Any omissions or errors of attribution or acknowledgement here or elsewhere are unintentional and will be corrected in future printings if notified in writing to the publisher.

Page 28: drawing of Professor Branestawm by Heath Robinson, reproduced by kind permission of the Estate of Mrs J. C. Robinson and Pollinger Limited. Copyright © the Estate of Mrs J. C. Robinson.

Pages 38–9: dichotomy descriptors for Sensing, Intuition, Judging and Perceiving. "Further information is available at www.cpp.com where you can purchase the *Introduction to Type®* booklet. Modified and reproduced by special permission of the Publisher, CPP, Inc., Mountain View, CA 94043 from *Introduction to Type*, 6th edition, by Isabel Briggs Myers. Copyright 1998 by Peter B. Myers and Katharine D. Myers. Al rights reserved. Further reproduction is prohibited without the Publisher's written consent."

Page 76: photograph of Remington typewriter. Getty Images.

Page 100: photograph of Newbury Bypass Protest. Copyright Tony Olmos 1996.

Page 124: photograph of polar bear. Reproduced with permission © Michael Bradley.

Page 154: photograph of Martin Luther King. Getty Images.

Page 178: photograph of teacups © Tom Bragg.

Page 192: photograph of Chinese woman with mobile phone © TTPCom Ltd, reproduced with permission.

Notes

1 See www.ttpgroup.com

2 See www.tcp-uk.co.uk

3 See www.stopclimatechaos.org and www.icount.org.uk

4 The exact quote is "quod non temere accidit" ("which cannot be by chance"). Francis Bacon, *Novum organon*, ed. Graham Rees. Oxford: Clarendon Press, 2004, p. 294.

5 The date of the creation of the world was a topic of great interest in the seventeenth century. The most widely accepted chronology was based primarily on an interpretive reading of the Bible by James Ussher, Bishop of Armagh (now in Northern Ireland). This became known as the Ussher-Lightfoot calendar. His careful calculations were based firstly on the detailed father-son lineage given in the Bible for the time from Adam to Solomon. Calculations for the second period were based on the durations of the reigns of the kings between Solomon and the Babylonian Captivity. Unfortunately, different versions of the Bible differed in specifying these, but he chose to base his work on the Hebrew version. The last period was the most difficult because the Bible gives no information until the birth of Jesus, so he had to try to link events described in the Bible to other historical events described by the Romans or the Persians. The result gave the time of creation as nightfall preceding 23 October 4004 BC. There were various other calendars around at the time, giving somewhat different dates. They were all fairly similar, because they were all using much the same methodology to calculate the result. It may be an accident that Ussher's remains well known, because from about 1700 on, annotated editions of the King James edition of the Bible began to refer to it.

6 Personal communication, Northern Foods, manufacturer of sandwiches for various major UK supermarkets.

7 Gregory A. Stevens and James Burley, "3,000 raw ideas=one commercial success!", *Research Technology Management* 40:3 (May–June1997), pp. 16–27.

8 R. Miller, *Continents in Collision*. Alexandria, VA: Time-Life Books, 1983, p. 51.

9 http://pubs.usgs.gov/gip/dynamic/historical.html

10 This is the idea that the earth's crust is broken up into a number of plates carrying the continents, which are believed to float on top of a thin layer of semi-fluid rock. The plates are bounded by areas like the Mid-Atlantic Ridge, where new crust is being created from within the planet, and other areas, such as the San Andreas Fault in California, where old crust is falling into trenches. This allows the continents to move as part of the plates, without needing to plough through the earth's crust (as Wegener had assumed, but which Harold Jeffreys, a noted English geophysicist, had shown would be physically impossible).

11 *American Journal of Science* 242 (1944), pp. 218–31. Available online at www. wku.edu/~smithch/biogeog/LONG1944.htm

12 www.whitehouse.gov/news/releases/2001/10/20011004-8.html

13 Luke 11:23, Matthew 12:30.

14 www.whitehouse.gov/news/releases/2001/11/20011110-3.html

15 Oxford Dictionary of English. Oxford: Oxford University Press, 2003, p. 860.

16 Sir Geoffrey Vickers. Only 21 at the time, he survived, and was awarded the Victoria Cross, Britain's highest award for gallantry

17 This term encompasses the various ways of owning and controlling ideas, e.g., patents, copyright, trademarks, trade secrets and even know-how. Copyright is the right, initially owned by the author, to control the reproduction of their work.

18 Personal communication, Prof. Edward Roberts. The five preconditions for successful internal venturing were: defined individual authority and responsibility; measurable results and recognition; emotional involvement and commitment; freedom from inhibitions and organizational constraints; and direct visibility to senior management.

19 Personal communication, Dr S. D. Noam Cook, Professor of Philosophy, San José State University.

20 www.ciadvertising.org/sa/spring_06/adv391k/jung326/paper/trends.html

21 Mark Earls, *Welcome to the Creative Age: Bananas, Business and the Death of Marketing*. Chichester: John Wiley & Sons Ltd, 2004, Chapter 3.

22 An interview with Al Ries, best-selling author of *The Fall of Advertising and the Rise of PR*, by Cincom's Expert Access Steve Kayser. Online at www. enewsbuilder.net/techimage/e_article000442814.cfm?x=b11,0,w

23 Alastair Barber, abc ltd, www.abcltd.uk.com

24 Excellent teachers' packs for a range of exercises are available from Careers Research Advisory Council at www.crac.org.uk.

25 www.bbc.co.uk/history/historic_figures/archimedes.shtml

26 For a clear explanation of the physics see Michio Kaku, www.mkaku.org or www.pbs.org/wgbh/nova/einstein/kaku.html

27 Tavistock Consultancy Service, www.tavistockconsultancyservice.com

28 Mark Hayhurst, "Special report: space exploration", *Guardian* (23 January 2001).

29 For more detailed information on the MBTI test or to find someone accredited to use it, see www.cpp.com, www.opp.co.uk or www.austpsychpress.com.au. MBTI and Myers-Briggs Type Indicator are the registered trademarks of the Myers-Briggs Type Indicator Trust.

30 Data from "Top Management Teams and Organizational Renewal" by D. K. Hurst et al. in *Creative Management*, ed. Jane Henry. London: Sage Publications Ltd, 1991.

31 Tables reproduced with permission from Isabel Briggs Myers, *Introduction to Type: A guide to understanding your results on the Myers-Briggs Type Indicator* ®. Mountain View, California: CPP, Inc. Sixth edition, pp. 9–10.

32 EU Mission to Japan on product innovation, 2000.

33 *MBTI® Manual: A Guide to the Development and Use of the Myers-Briggs Type Indicator*, third edition, 1998.

34 A million to one.

35 Greg A. Stevens and James Burley, "Piloting the Rocket of Radical Innovation", *Research-Technology Management* (March–April 2003), pp. 16–25.

36 "Type Development and Leadership Development Integrating Reality and Vision, Heart and Mind" by Catherine Fitzgerald in *Developing Leaders: Research and Applications in Psychological Type and Leadership Development*, ed. Catherine Fitzgerald and Linda K. Kirby. Mountain View, California: Davies-Black Publishing, 1997.

37 Ibid.

38 Note that all the terms "Creative Maverick", "Visionary Leader", etc., are ones that I find useful to help people grasp the implication of their Myers-Briggs Type, rather than official terminology used by the creators or publisher of the MBTI® assessment.

39 www.wired.com/wired/archive/4.09/czik.html

40 Mihaly Csikszentmihalyi, *Creativity: Flow and the Psychology of Discovery and Invention*. New York: HarperCollins Publishers, 1997, pp. 57–76. His ten dimensions of creativity are 1) Energetic and yet often quiet and at rest; 2) Smart, yet naive; 3) Playful yet disciplined; 4) Alternating between fantasy and reality; 5) Both extroverted and introverted behaviour; 6) Humble and yet proud; 7) Masculine and feminine; 8) Rebellious yet traditional; 9) Passionate yet objective; 10) Both suffering and enjoyment.

41 The distribution of type in a sample of US executives is as follows: NJ 37%, NP 29.8%, SJ 28.3%, SP 4.5%. In male US high school students, the equivalent figures are NJ 23.7%, NP 20%, SJ 45.5%, SP 10.7%. Data collated from Catherine Fitzgerald and Linda K. Kirby (eds), op. cit., p. 22.

42 Andreas Mavromatis, *Hypnagogia: The Unique State of Consciousness Between Wakefulness and Sleep*. London: Routledge and Kegan Paul, 1987.

43 Teresa Amabile et al., *Creativity in Context: Update to the Social Psychology of Creativity*. Oxford: Westview Press, 1996. p. 35. Her third condition is that it is "heuristic" not "algorithmic", i.e that there is no clearly defined path to the goal, and maybe no clearly defined goal at all.

44 www.ibiblio.org/wm

45 Mihaly Csikszentmihalyi, op. cit.

46 www.innocentive.com

47 Martha Augoustinos and Iain Walker, *Social Cognition: An Integrated Introduction*. London: Sage Publications, 2000, pp. 85–7.

48 In the biblical tradition, Jubilee was the "Sabbath of Sabbaths", a time that occurred every seven Sabbaths, or every 49 years. At Jubilee, slaves were to be set free, debts were to be forgiven, wealth was to be equitably and generously shared among all, and the land was to be given rest from its labour. There is no evidence that it ever happened, but the concept is central one in the Christian faith. For more detail see http://generalsynod.anglican.ca/ministries/departments/mm/1999/winter/mm09.html

49 See these, and some of his other work, on www.cockrill.org

50 I. Nonaka and H. Takeuchi, *The Knowledge-Creating Company: How Japanese Companies Create the Dynamics of Innovation*. New York: Oxford University Press, 1995, pp. 11–12.

51 BBC Radio 4, "Thought for the day", Revd Tom Butler, 14 November 2006.

52 Douglas Adams, *The Hitchhiker's Guide to the Galaxy*. London: Pan Books, 1979, p. 130.

53 J. W. Getzels and M. Csikszentmihalyi, *The Creative Vision: A longitudinal study of problem finding in art*. New York: Wiley, 1976.

54 A. Koestler, *The Act of Creation*. New York: Macmillan, 1964.

55 S. Freud, *Leonardo da Vinci: A study in sexuality*. New York: Brill, 1916.

56 Ronald A. Finke, Thomas B. Ward and Steven M. Smith, *Creative Cognition: Theory, Research and Applications*. Cambridge, Massachusetts: The MIT Press, 1996.

57 Ronald A. Finke, *Creative Imagery: Discoveries and Inventions in Visualisation*. Hillsdale, NJ: Erlbaum, 1990, pp. 252–7.

58 These were the 4-EPB vehicles, still in use on the Horsham line in about 1994.

59 www.femalehealth.com

60 The World Health Organization [WHO] criticized the Vatican's view as "dangerous" and "incorrect" in the face of "a global pandemic which has already killed more than 20 million people, and currently affects at least 42 million". They argued that "consistent and correct" condom use reduces the risk of HIV transmission by 90% and that "intact condoms … are essentially impermeable to the smallest STD virus". Steve Bradshaw, "Vatican: condoms don't stop Aids", *Guardian* (9 October 2003).

61 Personal communication, Peter Granger. www.inspired2lead.co.uk

62 "Maximum Magic" points are the times in a development when an idea is at its easiest to sell. Typically the first point of maximum magic is when the concept is clear, but the problems and disadvantages are not yet apparent. The second is when there's something that works and demonstrates the principle is valid, even if it doesn't look very beautiful or work perfectly. There is then usually a long haul until the third point of maximum magic when there's a fully working prototype that looks and works like the final product.

63 Mihaly Csikszentmihalyi, op. cit.

64 www.clearly.ca/files/aboutus.php

65 For more detail, see James M. Utterback, *Mastering the Dynamics of Innovation*. Boston: Harvard Business School Press, 1996.

66 Ivan D. Brown, Ivan Brown Associates, "Review of the 'Looked but Failed to See' Accident Causation Factor", *Road Safety Research Report No. 60*, Cambridge, November 2005, Department for Transport: London.

67 K. Rumar, "The Basic Driver Error: Late Detection", *Ergonomics* 33:10/11 (1990), pp. 1281–90.

68 D. J. Simons and C. F. Chabris, "Gorillas in Our Midst: Sustained Inattentional Blindness for Dynamic Events", *Perception 28* (1999), pp. 1059–74.

69 These demonstrations are available on http://viscog.beckman.uiuc.edu/media/mousetrap.html

70 D. E. Broadbent, "The Hidden Preattentive Process", *American Psychologist* 32 (1977), pp. 109–18.

71 For further discussion of this, and other strange effects, see Rita Carter, *Mapping the Mind*. London: Seven Dials, 1999, p. 125.

72 http://jeffmilner.com/backmasking.htm

73 The Galileo Project, Rice University. http://galileo.rice.edu/sci/observations/sunspots.html

74 In different contexts these are also known as schema, frames or social representations, but for simplicity I will in general call them all mental models.

75 Alexander Linklater, "The 7/7 Bomb Survivors' Tricks of Memory", *Guardian* (16 December 2006).

76 James A. Baker and Lee H. Hamilton, et al., *The Iraq Study Group Report*, p. 62. Available online at www.usip.org

77 Martha Augoustinos and Iain Walker, op. cit., p. 44.

78 S. T. Fiske, D. R. Kinder and W. M. Larter, "The Novice and the Expert: Knowledge Based Strategies in Political Cognition", *Journal of Experimental Social Psychology* 19: 4 (July 1983).

79 Ralph Katz and Thomas J. Allen, "Investigating the Not Invented Here (NIH) syndrome: A look at the performance, tenure, and communication patterns of 50 R&D Project Groups", *R&D Management* 12, 1, 1982, pp. 7–19.

80 C. Nemeth, "Managing Innovation, when less is more", *California Management Review* 40:1 (Fall 1997).

81 BBC News 24, 22 August 2006, http://news.bbc.co.uk/1/hi/
   business/5220856.stm

82 Ed Crooks, "Europeans 'would accept climate change curbs'", *Financial Times*
   (19 November 2006).

83 Pew Research Center, 12 July 2006, http://people-press.org/reports/pdf/280.
   pdf

84 Nancy Stauffer, MIT Laboratory for Energy and the Environment. Press release:
   "Climate change now Americans' #1 environmental concern, MIT survey
   finds", http://sequestration.mit.edu/research/survey2006.html

85 Pew Global attitudes project, June 2006, http://pewglobal.org/reports/display.
   php?PageID=827

86 Richard E. Nisbett, *The Geography of Thought: How Asians and Westerners Think
   Differently and Why.* London: Nicholas Brealey Publishing, 2005.

87 Jared Diamond, *Collapse.* London: Allen Lane, 2005, Chapters 7–8.

88 For more detail on the AIDS activists, see an excellent discussion in Chapter 7
   of *The Golem at Large* by Harry Collins and Trevor Pinch. Cambridge: Cambridge
   University Press, 2006. The chapter is based on research in S. Epstein, *Impure
   Science: AIDS, Activism and the Politics of Knowledge.* Berkeley, Los Angeles and
   London: University of California Press, 1996.

89 G. Lakoff et al., *Don't Think of an Elephant: Know Your Values and Frame the Debate.*
   White River Junction, Vermont: Chelsea Green Publishing, 2004.

90 Department of Health, press release 6 March 2007.

91 Richard E. Nisbett, op. cit., 2005, pp. 118–19.

92 Ibid. p. 228.

93 W. Chan Kim and Renée Mauborgne, "Tipping Point Leadership", *Harvard
   Business Review* (April 2003).

94 R. Weber and J. Crocker, "Cognitive Processes in the Revision of Stereotypical
   Beliefs," *Journal of Personality and Social Psychology* 45:5 (1983), pp. 961–77.

95 Acts 9:4–9:17.

96 Garry Wills, *What Paul Meant.* New York: Viking Penquin, 2006, pp. 125–6,
   summarised by Harvey Cox in Book World, *Washington Post*, 2006, www.
   amazon.com/What-Paul-Meant-Garry-Wills/dp/0670037931

97 Martha Augoustinos and Iain Walker, op. cit., p. 54.

98 www.eco-action.org/dod/no7/1-4.html

99 Dreadlocked Swampy first became famous when he dug himself into a tunnel
   on the route of the A30 at Fairmile near Honiton in South Devon. He
   subsequently became the public face of the activists, even appearing on a
   comedy programme (*Have I Got News for You*) and in fashion shoots.

100 Obituary, Richard Moog, BBC News, 22 August 2005, http://news.bbc.
    co.uk/1/hi/entertainment/music/4696651.stm

101 In the USA this means to sell one million records and hence get a framed platinum disc from the recording company.

102 www.realclimate.org/index.php/archives/2006/08/new-public-opinion-poll-on-global-warming

103 Jeff Hecht, "Global Warming May Pump Up Hurricane Power", *New Scientist* (1 August 2005).

104 Mark Kurlansky, *Nonviolence: 25 Lessons from the History of a Dangerous Idea*. London: Jonathan Cape, 2006, p. 20.

105 Fundamental Attribution Error, or FAE, is the tendency for people to overestimate the role of personal factors in controlling behaviour, and underestimate the importance of situational factors.

106 R. Weber and J. Crocker, "Cognitive Processes in the Revision of Stereotypical Beliefs", op. cit., 45:5 (1983), pp. 961–77.

107 Intergovernmental Panel on Climate Change, *Fourth Assessment Report*, 2007 summary for policy makers.

108 *Stern Review on the economics of climate change*. HM Treasury (January 2007), www.hm-treasury.gov.uk/independent_reviews/stern_review_economics_climate_change/sternreview_index.cfm

109 A good summary of some technological options is the stabilization wedges concept from Princeton University, see www.princeton.edu/~cmi/resources/stabwedge.htm

110 State of the Union address, 30 January 2007.

111 In 2006, Airbus pointed out that aviation is only 2% of global emissions, although this figure is forecast to grow at 5% p.a., and it ignores the radiative forcing effect which makes its contribution worse: www.rtcc.org/2006/html/soc_air_airbus.html

112 Tony Blair told the House of Commons Liaison Committee on 6 February 2007, "We are only 2% of global carbon emissions." This ignores the impact of the UK's imports and the financial services sector.

113 George W. Bush, 11 June 2001: www.whitehouse.gov/news/releases/2001/06/20010611-2.html

114 Bjørn Lomborg, "Why Kyoto will not stop this", *Guardian* (17 August 2001).

115 Patrick Barkham, "Cost of tourism: Oops, we helped ruin the planet", *Guardian* (4 March 2006).

116 See www.futura.com for their climate communication guides "The Rules of the Game" and "New Rules: New Game".

117 www.stopclimatechaos.org

118 Edgar H. Schein, *The Corporate Culture Survival Guide*. San Francisco: Jossey-Bass, 1999, Chapter 6.

119 Richard Feynman, *What Do You Care What Other People Think?* London: Unwin Paperbacks, 1990, pp. 179–88 and 220.

120 Kate Douglas, "Supersize This", *New Scientist* (27 January 2007), pp. 28–31.

121 In this 2004 film, Morgan Spurlock spent 30 days eating exclusively at McDonalds, never turning down an offer to "super size me". He gained 13% of his body weight in the process.

122 Chris Rose, *How to Win Campaigns: 100 Steps to Success*. London: Earthscan, 2005, pp. 10–12.

123 Thomas Kuhn, *The Structure of Scientific Revolutions*. Chicago: The University of Chicago Press, 1996, p. 68.

124 Union of Concerned Scientists, press release, 3 January 2007, www.ucsusa.org/news/press_release/ExxonMobil-GlobalWarming-tobacco.html

125 Lawrence W. Sherman and Heather Strang, *Restorative Justice: the evidence*. Available online at http://www.smith-institute.org.uk/publications.htm

126 Fred Pearce, "Look, no carbon footprint", *New Scientist* (9 March 2007).

127 See www.cultdyn.co.uk

128 Rosemary Randall, "A New Climate for Psychotherapy", *Psychotherapy and Politics International* 3.3 (September 2005). Available online at www.cambridgecarbonfootprint.org/docs/new_climate_psychotherapy.pdf

129 Larry Hirschhorn, *The Workplace Within: Psychodynamics of Organizational Life*. Cambridge, Massachusetts: The MIT Press, 1990, pp.164–71.

130 Helen Carter, "Nurse gets five years for seeking to kill two patients", *Guardian* (19 June 2004).

131 Peter Dosoch, "When Bullfighting's in the Blood", *Psychology Today* (September/October 1994). Online at http://psychologytoday.com/articles/pto-19940901-000015.htm

132 http://psychologytoday.com/conditions/agoraphobia.html

133 www.energist-international.com

134 Fumio Kodama, *Emerging Patterns of Innovation: Sources of Japan's Technological Edge*. Boston: Harvard Business School Press,1995, pp. 57–61.

135 2006 figure at http://www.inteletex.com/NewsDetail.asp?PubId=&NewsId=5145

136 Dean Radin, *The Conscious Universe: The Scientific Truth of Psychic Phenomena*. New York: HarperCollins Publishers, 1997, p. 84.

137 Dean Radin, "Thinking about Telepathy", *Journal of the Royal Institute of Philosophy* 3 (Spring 2003).

138 One example is the Nobel Prize-winner Professor Brian Josephson of the University of Cambridge. www.tcm.phy.cam.ac.uk/~bdj10/

139 H. E. Puthoff, Ph.D, "CIA-Initiated Remote Viewing at Stanford Research Institute", Institute for Advanced Studies at Austin: www.remoteviewinghistory.com/cia-remote-viewing-at-stanford-research-institute.html

140 Personal communication. See also www.sheldrake.org/D&C/controversies/dogmaticscepticism.html. For a more detailed discussion of skepticism in parapsychology see www.skepticalinvestigations.org

141 3D turbulent flow is particularly hard to model, as is the transition from the more gentle "laminar" flow.

142 I have twice watched dowsers at work: both times they were successful. The first was in the 1960s, finding a water supply for Oundle School's swimming pool; the second was in the late 1990s, when engineers were checking the position of electricity cables before trenching work on Melbourn Science Park.

143 For the full text, see www.americanrhetoric.com/speeches/mlkihaveadream.htm

144 For the full text, see www.historyplace.com/speeches/churchill-hour.htm

145 1 ltd, www.1limited.com

146 http://news.bbc.co.uk/1/hi/magazine/6314837.stm

147 Great Eastern Investment Forum, Cambridge.

148 Chun Wei Choo, The Knowing Organization: How Organizations Use Information to Construct Meaning, Create Knowledge and Make Decisions. New York: Oxford University Press, 1998.

149 Teresa Lloyd, "Why Rich People Give", Philanthopy UK. Summary available from www.philanthropyuk.org

150 Edward R. Tufte, Visual Explanations, images and quantities, evidence and narrative, Cheshire Connecticut: Graphics Press, 1998, p. 42. They originally appeared in The Report of the Presidential Commission on the Space Shuttle Challenger Accident, Washington, DC: 1986, Volume IV, pp. 664–73.

151 For an excellent detailed discussion of the presentation of information in the Challenger disaster see Edward R. Tufte, Visual Explanations: Images and Quantities, Evidence and Narrative. Ibid., pp. 39–53.

152 Denise Chong, The Girl in the Picture: The Remarkable Story of Vietnam's Most Famous Casualty. London: Simon and Schuster, 2001.

153 www.kimfoundation.com/en/

154 www.snopes.com/religion/soulweight.asp

155 Stephen Denning, The Springboard: How Story-telling Ignites Action in Knowledge-era Organizations. Boston: Butterworth Heinemann, 2001, p. 9.

156 www.peacedirect.org

157 www.peacedirect.org/latest-news/Practical_Peace.html

158 For an excellent detailed discussion of the London Congestion Charge see Martin G. Richards, Congestion Charging in London: The Policy and the Politics. Basingstoke: Palgrave Macmillan, 2005.

159 "Road Charging Options for London: A Technical Assessment" (hence ROCOL), Government Office for London, March 2000.

160 C. Wickens, Engineering Psychology and Human Performance. Columbus, OH: Merrill, 1984.

161 "Circles of Support and Accountability in the Thames Valley: The first three years, April 2002 to March 2005", *Quaker Peace and Social Witness* (August 2005).

162 *New Scientist* 2583 (23 December 2006), p. 30.

163 Steven Weber, *The Success of Open Source*. Cambridge Massachusetts: Harvard University Press, 2004, pp.134–49.

164 Message Labs, press release 13 December 2006.

165 Note that the terms World Wide Web and Internet are not synonymous, although they are often confused. The World Wide Web is a set of interconnected documents and files, linked by the hyperlinks. The Internet is a set of computers, linked together by copper wire, WiFi links etc. For a detailed discussion of the difference, and Tim Berners-Lee's role, see http://en. wikipedia.org/wiki/Internet and http://en.wikipedia.org/wiki/World_Wide_ Web

166 *Proceedings of the National Academy of Sciences* 100, p. 3531.

167 *Nature* 425, p. 785.

168 www.answersingenesis.org/tj/v14/i1/galileo.asp

169 A. Koestler, *The Sleepwalkers: A History of Man's Changing Vision of the Universe*. London: Hutchinson, 1959, p. 425.

170 For more detail see www.marshallfoundation.org/library/marshall_and_the_ plan.html

171 www.developments.org.uk/articles/loose-talk-saves-lives

172 Reuters Market Light. Personal communication, Amanda West, Reuters.

173 The theorem was proposed by the seventeenth-century mathematician Pierre de Fermat. It states: If an integer n is greater than 2, then $a^n + b^n = c^n$ has no solutions in non-zero integers a, b and c. Tantalizingly for mathematicians for the next 350 years, he wrote in the margin of one of his books: "I have a truly marvellous proof of this proposition which this margin is too narrow to contain."

174 "Never doubt that a small group of thoughtful committed citizens can change the world" is a registered trademark of The Institute for Intercultural Studies, Inc., New York, and is used with their permission. The source of this famous quotation is unclear, but The Institute of Intercultural Studies suggests that "it probably came into circulation through a newspaper report of something said spontaneously and informally. We know, however, that it was firmly rooted in her professional work and that it reflected a conviction that she expressed often, in different contexts and phrasing."

Index

Page references in *italics* indicate illustrations

About the author

Anne Miller is an authority on creativity and innovation, with an infectious enthusiasm for ideas, and the expertise to help make them reality. She started her career with an MA in Engineering from Cambridge University, then spent 20 years leading teams developing innovative products for the world's leading companies. She is one of the world's most prolific female inventors, with 39 patents for a diverse range of products, ranging from power tools and medical products to the manufacturing system for the Femidom (the female condom).

In 1988 she was a co-founder of The Technology Partnership (now one of Europe's leading technology innovation organizations) and in 2000 founded The Creativity Partnership, providing consulting and training for some of the world's most successful organizations. She is also a board member of Stop Climate Change, a coalition of over 90 of the UK's leading non-governmental organizations demanding action on climate change.

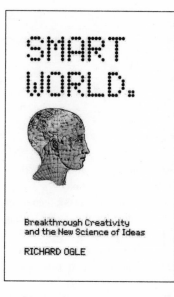

Breakthrough Creativity
and the New Science of Ideas

RICHARD OGLE

Smart World

Breakthrough Creativity and the
New Science of Ideas

Richard Ogle

What do jazz musician Dave Brubeck, Apple's Steve Jobs, Mattel's Ruth Handler and architect Frank Gehry all have in common? They are credited with some of the most inventive accomplishments of the past half-century – the classic jazz album *Time Out*, the iPod, Barbie and Spain's spectacular Guggenheim Museum. Yet their creative leaps all came about differently. They each combined their individual imaginative intelligence with unique networks of ideas that lay outside their own minds to reach true breakthroughs in their fields.

Clearly, not all brilliant innovations originate only from the minds of individual geniuses. On the contrary, our world is made up of intelligent networked spaces that, if we navigate them skilfully, can lead us to generate unprecedented ideas.

Welcome to *Smart World*. In this provocative book, Richard Ogle argues that creative breakthroughs are born when individuals and groups access new *idea-spaces* and exploit the principles that govern them. Boldly outlining a new science of ideas, he sets out nine laws – including "hotspots," "the fit get fitter" and "small-world networks" – that govern idea-spaces. And he illuminates each law with fascinating stories of dramatic breakthroughs in science, business and art.

Anyone interested in how creative leaps occur – primarily in business, but also in science, technology, and the arts – will value this book, as will those interested in how human imagination, intuition, and insight *really* operate.

Insightful and compelling, *Smart World* will forever transform the way we think about creativity and innovation.

ISBN 978–0–462–09921–0 / £18.99 Hardback